Led by Light:

How to develop your intuitive mediumship abilities

Book One: Unfolding

Led by Light:

How to develop your intuitive mediumship abilities

Book One: Unfolding

Rev. Joanna Bartlett

Publisher's Cataloging-in-Publication Data

Names: Bartlett, Joanna.
Title: Led by light : how to develop your intuitive mediumship abilities : book 1, unfolding / Rev. Joanna Bartlett.
Other titles: Unfolding.
Description: Eugene, OR : Alight Press, 2016. | Series: Led by light, bk. 1.
Identifiers: LCCN 2016917419 | ISBN 978-1-945489-04-4 (pbk.) | ISBN 978-1-945489-05-1 (ebook)
Subjects: LCSH: Mediums. | Psychic ability. | Intuition. | Spiritualism. | Guides (Spiritualism) | BISAC: BODY, MIND & SPIRIT / Channeling & Mediumship. | BODY, MIND & SPIRIT / Spiritualism. | BODY, MIND & SPIRIT / Parapsychology / ESP (Clairvoyance, Precognition, Telepathy).
Classification: LCC BF1286 .B37 2016 (print) | LCC BF1286 (ebook) | DDC 133.9/1--dc23.

Alight Press LLC
2075 Charnelton St.
Eugene, OR 97405
www.alightpress.com
Printed in the United States of America

Contents

Introduction

How I became a professional Spiritualist intuitive medium

Did I choose mediumship or did mediumship choose me?

I never intended to become a medium. Most of us don't. It's just who we are. If I ever write a tell-all mediumship memoir, it'll probably be called *The Reluctant Medium*. Because even now there are days I wonder why I do what I do. Every time I question if it's the path I'm supposed to be on (I'm a bit of a questioner), I ask Spirit to show me the way forward. And this is the path I keep coming back to.

My mediumship story starts out when I was a little kid, although I didn't know it at the time.

When I first began learning about mediumship, I'd hear experienced mediums talk about how they always had this ability, ever since they were a small child. "Not me," I thought. "I don't remember talking to any dead people."

But as I learned more about mediumship and developed my own abilities, the memories came back. I specifically remember someone I used to see in our breakfast room, often by the hallway that led to the downstairs bathroom and garage. He was familiar to me and I knew this person was male. I knew he was related. And he used to talk to me, although I no longer remember what he said.

Looking back now, I believe he was my brother, Anthony, who died when I was 2 years old. He was 17, practically an adult, especially to a little kid. I've often felt him close to me throughout the years—and have received messages from him through other mediums. And, logistically, it makes sense. I was very young, so I was open to hearing and seeing Spirit and he wanted to check in with all of us.

I soon learned, though, not to talk about ghosts. "There's no such thing as ghosts," was the forceful answer I received when I told my parents.

And so, for the most part, I stopped seeing them. Or at least admitting that I could.

As a teenager, I realized I sensed and felt things my peers didn't. I could tell when someone was lying. I knew what people's intentions really were. Did I listen to my inner knowing? Not often, but it still spoke to me. I knew where people hurt—and could relieve their pain by taking it on myself (this is not the recommended method, by the way). For the most part, I tried to ignore these feelings and knowings and push them away.

When I was a young adult, I finally found a community ready and able to teach me about my gifts. In that sense, I didn't choose to become a medium—I always was one—so it's not a matter of wanting to be one or not. I did, however, choose to pursue developing my gifts, instead of continuing to repress and ignore them to the best of my ability.

As far as actively practicing and demonstrating mediumship, that snuck up on me. The community I found to study and grow in was a small Spiritualist church. It didn't have its own church building and instead met in a very church-like room at the Days Inn on the corner of East and Alexander streets in Rochester, N.Y.

There were only a handful of people at some services, usually not more than 15. Getting up to give messages—after taking a church-sponsored mediumship class, of course—wasn't terribly intimidating. It was a warm, inviting, supportive atmosphere. I also attended whatever mediumship classes and meditation circles the church offered and knew almost all the people, on some level, that I gave messages to. I also learned how to perform spiritual healing, which put me in direct contact with people I would then give messages to at the end of the church service.

Over time, the church grew. We purchased a building of our own and I actively worked on public relations to increase our congregation and event attendance. We added more events, such as a monthly All Message Service, where mediums gave out readings gallery-style, offering short five-minute readings to each person in attendance. Our efforts were successful. People streamed in through the doors. But we didn't have a whole lot of strong, practicing mediums.

So I became a medium largely out of necessity—right at the time I began a mediumship certification course through Morris Pratt Institute (the educational arm of the National Spiritualist Association of Churches).

I also felt a large push by my own loved ones in Spirit, who I swear were dancing around my home office the night after I received Lesson 1 in the mail. It was the same day I came back from offering healing at an All Message Service with the realization that the following month I'd be offering mediumship readings instead.

That was the push I needed to begin regularly practicing mediumship at church services and special events such as All Message Services and psychic fairs.

Demonstrating mediumship developed into teaching it. As I continued my mediumship and ministerial certification, I became a student minister, and, among other things, spearheaded the re-establishment of the church's mediumship certification program. This certification program taught student mediums how to give out messages properly in a church service (we call it platform decorum) and helped them strive for evidential messages. I mentored student mediums and taught a yearly mediumship refresher course for all the church's mediums.

At that point, you'd think I was in it for life, right? Apparently not, or at least I didn't know it yet.

By the time I became a nationally-certified medium and an ordained minister, I had two young kids. I was so determined to finish my studies and get to the end goal that, when my daughter was only a week old, I traveled two hours to the Lily Dale Spiritualist community and the NSAC headquarters to take my oral examinations in front of the National Spiritualist Association of Churches board of directors. I left my 1-year-old son at home with my mother, but my daughter came along for the ride and her father took her for a stroller ride around Lily Dale while I did my exam. I like to think I passed on my own merits, but I'm sure letting the board members hold my sweet week-old baby didn't hurt.

Around the same time, my church was undergoing upheaval. I knew I either needed to step in and give it my time and energy, or step away. I didn't have the energy to give it—I developed postpartum depression, my marriage was presented with a significant challenge and the details of surviving everyday life with two kids consumed me. So I stepped away. And with it, largely closed the door to my mediumship abilities for several years.

It wasn't until I'd moved to Eugene, Oregon (fortunately, I still listened to my intuition when it came through loud and clear), divorced my children's father and been laid-off from an engrossing career in marketing communications that it opened back up.

There weren't, and still aren't at the time I'm writing this book, any Spiritualist churches in Eugene, but I'd snagged a ticket to see James Van Praagh when he was in town. As I sat in the audience, listening to him talk about Spiritualism and mediumship—its purpose and its effect on his own life—something inside me opened up. The urge to be open again was insistent and loud. I didn't get a message from James that night, but I certainly heard the message from Spirit.

After visiting friends in Rochester, N.Y., later that same summer, and complaining that there weren't any Spiritualist churches or circles or classes in Eugene, I got another message: start your own.

I told Spirit I wasn't sure about the whole thing. It seemed like an unlikely career path, after all. Before that, I'd been a career woman with the ambition to keep moving up the ladder until I got to the top. It was a job I could easily talk about at social gatherings. Now I was going to be a medium? Really? But when I closed my eyes and meditated, it's what I heard to do.

So I did, one small step at a time. I began a twice-monthly drop-in development circle. Which led to offering readings and energy healing from my home. Since then, my intuitive mediumship work has continued to grow and blossom in ways I'd never even considered when I first created my website and put it out there that I was available for readings. I'm now teaching classes, mentoring students and holding public gallery readings again, as well as writing books about mediumship and spiritual development.

My agreement then, as it still is now, is that I'll do what's mine to do. I'll allow the path to unfold naturally and with ease. I won't push it. I won't fight it. I'll just be on it and see where it goes, with an open heart, wonder and curiosity. And I'll share what I know and learn with others, so they can find their way also.

What this book can do for you

When I decided to study mediumship, it was because I needed to learn about and understand what was going on with my abilities. Perhaps the same is true for you—whether your mediumship abilities are bursting forth uncontrollably and uncomfortably, or whether they're still quiet and latent. If you have the urge to learn more about your intuition and mediumship, it's because there's something within you that's drawn to it. You're not making it up.

This is the first book in a series of two books about intuitive mediumship—what it is, how it works, how to develop it, how to use it personally and professionally.

Introduction

This book covers the foundation for developing and controlling your mediumship abilities. Along with a look at what intuitive mediumship is, how it works and what its purpose is, you'll learn how to consciously open and close yourself to Spirit and how to meditate, as well as how to raise your vibration and keep yourself grounded. Those last two might sound contradictory, but they're actually not.

You'll also learn about your intuition and how to connect with it, as well as how to meet and develop a relationship with your spirit guides. Finally, you'll start working with symbols and learn how to understand and interpret the messages you receive from Spirit.

I'm approaching this series of books as if you will, at some point, be doing intuitive mediumship readings for others. Perhaps for friends and family members. Perhaps in a circle or group. Perhaps professionally. But your starting point can be wherever it is that you are right now. You can only start from where you are, after all.

This first book lays the foundation—so if you're interested in learning about your abilities, read on. If they feel uncomfortable or like you're not in control, I'll teach you how to quiet things down. If you feel like you've got some kind of ability, but it's not clear or loud enough, I'll teach you how to open things up.

The most important thing to know is that this doesn't have to be scary or take over your life. You can go only as quickly as the slowest part of you feels safe to go. You don't need to rush anything. It'll all come in the time it's supposed to.

Know that you are held in love, that your highest and best good is yours, and all is well.

Chapter 1:
What is intuitive mediumship?

I use the term intuitive mediumship for the work I do. What does that mean?

In short, it's a type of mediumship in which I primarily use my intuition to access and understand information from Spirit in order to help people on their path in life.

Mediumship is the communication between those in Spirit and those in the physical plane of existence (like you, reading this book). Essentially, it bridges the gap between the seen and the unseen, the physical and the etheric, the known and the unknown. A person who can do this type of communication is a medium.

Intuition, which I'll devote chapter 7 to later on, is your direct connection with your higher self and with the energy of all that is, which Spiritualists call Infinite Intelligence and is your understanding of God.

When I tell people that I'm an intuitive medium and they look at me quizzically, I give them the short version, "I talk to dead people."

Intuitive mediumship is that, and more.

When I do readings, I use all of my intuitive, or psychic, senses to connect with my client's energy and divine self and access the information that's useful to them, that they need to know at that moment, for their highest and best good. Through my intuitive senses, I'm able to see, hear, smell, taste, feel and know information as well as connect with their loved ones in Spirit.

Types of mediumship

Mediumship falls into two main categories: *mental mediumship* and *physical mediumship.*

The main difference between mental and physical mediumship is where the energy and phenomena originate in your body. Mental mediumship is said to originate from the base of your brain, the center of your cerebrospinal nervous system. Physical mediumship phenomena are said to be centered in the solar plexus, which controls your sympathetic nervous system.

There's also a difference in whether the information is available to everyone present or only the medium. In mental mediumship, the information comes through the medium's mind and senses, and they are the only person who receives the information—although in the best case, the person receiving the message also feels an emotional connection to their loved one in Spirit. In physical mediumship, everyone present should be able to observe the phenomena as it occurs.

Mental mediumship

Mental mediumship is the most common form of mediumship in use today. Intuitive mediumship falls under mental mediumship. It uses the mental faculties (the mind) and intuitive senses (closely related to our physical senses of sight, sound, smell, taste and touch, as well as intuitive knowing).

Ways in which information comes through in mental mediumship include:

- **Clairvoyance**—intuitive or psychic seeing and vision
- **Clairaudience**—intuitive or psychic hearing
- **Clairalience**—intuitive or psychic smelling
- **Clairgustance**—intuitive or psychic tasting

- **Clairsentience**—intuitive or psychic feeling and sensing
- **Claircognizance**—intuitive or psychic knowing, direct knowledge from Spirit

The quality and clarity of the information that comes through from Spirit in this type of mediumship is dependent on the medium's own outlook, character, integrity and mental and emotional clarity. The clearer you are in your life and your intentions, the better messages you get from Spirit. I'll go into raising or clearing your vibration in chapter 6.

Information from Spirit often comes through using more than one of these clairsenses—seeing and smelling, for instance, or hearing a voice or word and getting a feeling or emotion associated with it as well.

A full explanation of these different types of mental mediumship and how to practice them are in the second book of this series.

Physical mediumship

Physical mediumship used to be extremely popular, but is generally less practiced today. There are some folks who are good, strong physical mediums, but it's also been the area with the most fraud and skepticism. As fewer people practice and teach it, the more it goes out of favor as there are fewer people who know how to do it and who can, in turn, teach others.

During physical mediumship, through a reaction between the entity in Spirit and the medium's own body, energy-based or ectoplasm-based phenomena are created which can be seen, heard or felt by everyone who is around.

Physical mediumship phenomena include:

- **Transfiguration**—the appearance of faces and figures in front of the medium's face and body
- **Direct voice**—in which voices from Spirit are heard by means of a voice box being formed from ectoplasm, often through the use of a mediumship trumpet
- **Table tipping**—the movement of a table in response to questions asked of those in Spirit
- **Trance mediumship and channeling**—in which the medium goes into a trance state and allows a noncorporeal entity (someone in Spirit) to enter and animate their physical body

15

- **Automatic writing and automatic drawing**—often done while the medium holds a pen and paper, or has their hands on a keyboard, and directly channels information from spirit in written or art form
- **Apportation**—the movement of objects, often through solid objects such as walls and doors
- **Independent slate writing**—in which two slates are bound together with chalk or lead in the middle for Spirit to produce written messages

My book, *Spirit Energy*, covers all these aspects of physical mediumship and how to practice them.

A brief history of mediumship

Mediumship has existed, in one form or another, as long as there have been people on this Earth.

It's been recorded in history throughout the ages. In 1,000 B.C., the ancient Greeks consulted oracles for answers. The Romans called mediums "soothsayers" and often sought their wisdom. Even the Bible mentions occurrences of clairaudience in II Kings 6:12, Mark 9:2-4 and Acts 9:4-7.

In later centuries, European royalty called upon their personal mediums, known as "stargazers."

Sadly for all us sensitive folk, in the 1600s, the church outlawed mediumship. Only priests were allowed to communicate with God and spirit. Everyone else was put to death (if caught).

However, in the late 1800s, being able to communicate with those in Spirit was no longer a reason to be labeled as a witch and killed. It began to become recognized as a desirable psychic power or ability.

Modern Spiritualism began with the mediumship of the Fox Sisters. On March 31, 1848, Margaretta and Catherine Fox communicated, through a devised series of raps and knocks, with the spirit of Charles B. Rosna, a peddler who had been murdered and buried in the cellar of their house. The Fox Sisters held demonstrations in Rochester, N.Y., and went on to travel extensively to spread Spiritualism.

Much of the mediumship in early Modern Spiritualism was physical mediumship. The earliest records of modern Spiritualism describe demonstrations of materialization and dematerialization.

Chapter 1: What is intuitive mediumship?

In the late 1800s, it was also common to receive messages from Spirit through automatic or independent writing. Isaac and Amy Post, a couple who befriended the Fox Sisters at the beginning of their careers, were both proficient at automatic writing. Amy Post became known as the Mother of Modern Spiritualism.

This early physical mediumship began by receiving messages as raps or through table tipping, spelling out messages with the table's noises or movements. This was followed by the planchette—a pencil attached to a board on wheels that was rolled over a piece of paper to spell out answers to questions asked by the sitters. The planchette developed into today's Ouija board.

Another example of the early physical mediumship of Modern Spiritualism is Daniel Dunglas Home who was well known for levitating—himself and the objects around him—and for not commercializing his mediumship. He was known as the Greatest Physical Medium in the History of Spiritualism.

Others experimented with slate writing, such as William Stainton Moses, Francis W. Monck and Henry Slade. In this form of mediumship, two slates are bound together with a piece of chalk in between them. During a séance or meditation, spirit entities move the chalk against the slates to create drawings or write messages. Several examples are on display in the museum at Lily Dale, N.Y.

In the early 1900s, mediums such as Pearl Curran began developing mediumship skills in automatic writing. Pearl Curran channeled Patience Worth and received a Pulitzer Prize for one of her novels.

Along with independent and automatic writing there were similar phenomena in direct painting, sketching and music. Lizzie and May Bangs were well known for their direct spirit paintings and several of their portraits are displayed in Lily Dale, N.Y., along with other examples of physical mediumship.

As Spiritualism and subsequent demonstrations of mediumship became increasingly popular so, too, did fraud. Some people sought to capitalize on the interest in physical phenomena and were willing to produce it, however they could, whether or not it was real. Plus, physical mediumship phenomena can take an enormous amount of energy on the part of the medium and is not always something that can be produced on demand. While it's clearly not OK for anyone to fraudulently create mediumship phenomena of any kind, it is understandable why some formerly reputable mediums chose to do so. In addition, in an increasingly skeptical, demanding environment, it becomes more difficult to produce genuine physical phenomena.

As a result, most of today's mediums demonstrate mental mediumship—most often clairvoyance, clairaudience and clairsentience. There are few teachers of physical phenomena and few public demonstrations.

For a time, interest in mediumship waned and so did the congregations of Spiritualist churches. However, with the recent surge popularity of famous mediums such as John Edward, James Van Prague, Sylvia Brown, Monica the Medium, the Long Island Medium and others, sincere interest in mediumship is again growing.

What is a medium?

The word *medium* gives rise to a host of puns: small medium at large, the happy medium, etc. But, in terms of Spiritualist mediumship, it refers to someone who's sensitive to vibrations from Spirit.

By using their intuitive senses, a medium can connect with Spirit energy and bring through information from loved ones, pets and spirit guides. They do this by tuning into the particular vibration or frequency of the being they are communicating with while also connecting with the universal energy of Infinite Intelligence and their own inner divinity.

The National Spiritualist Association of Churches defines a medium as:

> "One whose organism is sensitive to vibrations from the spirit world and through whose instrumentality, intelligences in that world are able to convey messages and produce the phenomena of Spiritualism."

I tell my clients that I am literally a medium—a conduit through which communication can pass, much like electricity through a wire.

Both the dictionary definitions of the noun, *medium*, are applicable to Spiritualist mediumship.

> An agency or means of doing something—the means, method, way, form, agency, avenue, channel, vehicle, instrument or mechanism.

> The intervening substance through which impressions are conveyed to the senses.

In the first definition, the medium is the instrument through which communication happens. And in the second definition, a medium is the substance through which impressions from Spirit are conveyed to those living. Both of these things happen during mediumship.

Messages given and received through mediumship should be helpful, uplifting and evidential. If you're receiving a reading, you should know who the medium is connecting with in Spirit through the information they give you about that person (or pet's) personality, physical description, how they died or some other piece of identifying information (that's the evidential part). The message should leave you feeling good. It should bring relief and release (uplifting). And it should be useful to you in your life.

Psychic, medium or something else?

Different mediums call themselves psychic mediums, intuitive mediums or spirit mediums. Or some combination of all of these. Or perhaps just psychic or intuitive. I've determined that I'm an intuitive spirit medium.

What's the difference?

Here are my general definitions.

Psychic refers to connecting with the energy of the person and reading what's going on with them, often related to their daily lives and concerns with finances, relationships, career and family who are still alive.

Mediumship refers specifically to communication with people who were once alive and are now deceased, as well as spirit guides. Pure mediumship connects directly to this energy and pretty much only that.

Intuition is a direct connection with Spirit, which is the energy that makes up all that exists in this universe. Developing your intuition, your connection with your higher self and your understanding of God or Spirit, is the first step in developing good psychic and mediumship skills. When I use my intuition during readings, I sense a push and pull of energy or a feeling of resistance or flow.

So, a person can be a psychic, able to tune into the energy attached to a person (or pet, place or object), or they can be intuitive and connect with information coming from Spirit about a person (or pet, place or object). Or they can be a medium and connect with people or pets in Spirit and bring through information.

Or they can be any combination.

Mediums are often psychic and intuitive. Developing intuitive and psychic skills are the first steps in opening up to and understanding your mediumship abilities.

Psychics are sometimes mediums as well, although they may not always be aware of it.

Many religions and philosophies, including Spiritualism, attempt to classify and rank these different abilities, with one being better than the other. Spiritualism lauds mediumship above all else, defining the difference between psychic and medium as this: a psychic taps into the vibrations of the universe, whereas a medium also attunes to spirit entities. Other religions, such as the Science of Mind, say that psychics are only picking up on the energy associated and attached to people, rather than the universe as a whole.

Chapter 1: What is intuitive mediumship?

Intuitives will often profess intuition to be the more important skill than psychic ability. And, psychics will proclaim their abilities to be a step up from intuition. Does it really matter? Is there a definitive answer? My answer to both is: probably not. It's all information. And if you're taking the steps outlined in the rest of this book—asking for the highest and best good for everyone involved, grounding yourself, setting boundaries, being aware of your filters, and working on raising your vibration—you'll get good information.

This book primarily covers intuitive mediumship. However, the information and exercises can be helpful if you're interested in developing only psychic and/or intuitive abilities as well. Most of the time, they tend to blend together.

Here's how I think of it:

Everything in this universe is made up of energy.

You can deliberately connect with the energy of other people, their worldly concerns, the truth of who they are, and their connections with those they love and who love them. That's psychic, intuitive and mediumship abilities all rolled together.

How mediumship works

Mediumship is governed by several natural laws—the laws that govern how everything in this universe works.

You're familiar with the law of gravity: what goes up must come down. That's a natural law. The theory of gravity is actually extremely complex, as I discovered when my daughter wanted to learn about gravity as her science fair project when she was in Kindergarten. We kept it simple and did some experiments to prove gravity exists (she jumped off the couch repeatedly and attempted to walk up the wall). Everyone understands how gravity affects their life, even if you don't understand the underlying principles of how it works. The rest of the natural laws also work whether or not you understand them. They also work absolutely—there's no getting around them.

The natural laws that govern mediumship are the laws of *vibration, attraction* and *continuity*. Much like the law of gravity, these natural laws are complex and entire books could be written about them. Here's a brief explanation of each.

The law of vibration

Here's the short story: Everything in the universe exists in a state of vibration. It's all about the frequency at which it vibrates.

Everything in this universe is made up of energy. Quantum science is showing us this—at the subatomic level, everything is energy.

This energy is in a constant state of motion. It moves and vibrates. The speed at which it vibrates is its frequency and different things vibrate at different frequencies. You're vibrating at a different frequency than the air you breathe or the book or e-reader you're holding as you read these words.

Even things that appear to be solid and still are vibrating. Their subatomic particles are bouncing around all over the place, but it's on a level at which you can't see it, so you believe that the object is solid.

The frequency at which a thing vibrates governs the form that the energy that makes up the thing will take. Everything has its own frequency and there's an infinite number of frequencies. It's true, some things have similar frequencies—each of the tables at the coffee shop where I often write vibrates at about the same frequency. They're all similar tables, after all.

27

And each person—in physical form or not—vibrates at their own frequency as well. While you go around with the belief that you're a solid, separate being, you're really made up of the same energy as everything else in the universe, vibrating madly at the subatomic level. It's the outward expression of that energy, governed by the frequency at which it vibrates, that makes you think you're separate and different. But you're not.

And this is the underpinning of how mediumship works. You're essentially connecting with the specific frequency of the people you read and their loved ones and, by tuning into that frequency, you're able to access information. This information is available because we're all made of the same fundamental energy.

The law of vibration governs the types of spirit entities you're able to communicate with through mediumship. As you work to increase your awareness, mental and emotional clarity and raise your own vibration, you're able to communicate with spirits and guides of higher vibrations. Raising your vibration also works in life in general, as it draws to you the people and experiences that match your vibration (which are more pleasant and enjoyable).

This is due to the next law, the law of attraction.

The law of attraction

A lot of people are generally familiar with this law. The law of attraction states that like attracts like. According to Ester Hicks' channeling of Abraham, "The Law of Attraction says: *That which is like unto itself is drawn*" (from *Ask and it is Given, Learning to Manifest Your Desires*).

The law of attraction applies to everything and is governed by our thoughts and inspired by our emotions. If you want to bring through Spirit intelligences of a high vibration then you must ask for this and believe it will be so. That's why you'll learn to ask to bring through the highest and best good. By holding this as your thought as you open to Spirit, this is all you attract and allow to communicate with and through you.

By continuing to educate yourself about mediumship, natural law, Spiritualism and its phenomena, you attract those in Spirit—and in the physical world—who are also educated and can help you further your education. By seeking and actively working to be a better person, to be more inspired and use that inspiration and understanding in our daily lives, you attract those to you who are likewise.

The law of attraction applies to both your physical and spiritual life, due to the law of continuity.

The law of continuity

The law of continuity governs all laws and is applied to both the physical and spiritual spectrums.

The Morris Pratt Institute's *Educational Course on Modern Spiritualism* says, "There is no break between physical and spiritual law...the law covers the entire spectrum of being to include both matter and spirit."

There is only one continuous spectrum of natural law that applies to everything in the spiritual and physical universes. This natural law is referenced in the Bible in a couple of places including the Lord's Prayer in Matthew 6:10 as "thy will be done on earth as it is in heaven" as well as the Hermetic saying, "as above, so below; as within, so without; as the universe, so the soul."

The law of continuity means that natural laws apply in all cases, everywhere. When it comes to setting your intentions, which you'll read more about in chapter 4, this is a very useful thing.

Chapter 2:
The purpose of
mediumship

So we've covered what intuitive mediumship is, its different types, some of its history and how it works. But what's the point of it? Why would you want to talk to dead people? Why is this an ability you might want to develop?

What mediumship brings

Mediumship isn't a party trick. It's not supposed to be a spectacle or a side show. And, while it does show that life continues on after the death of the physical body, its real purpose isn't to prove anything to anyone.

Infinite Intelligence doesn't need you to believe in it for it to continue to exist. Neither do your loved ones in Spirit. They're there, whether or not you know it or accept it.

So if the true purpose of mediumship isn't to prove the continuity of life or to further a religion,

why does it exist? Mediumship and the messages received through mediumship brings us healing,
knowledge and connection with Spirit.

Mediumship brings healing

Death is hard. Knowing your loved ones continue
on and can communicate with you eases grief. As a
medium, when you can bring through evidential information (meaning that the person receiving the
message can identify who it's coming from), it can
provide profound healing.

I still remember the first message I gave someone
that I received confirmation about. It was during a
Spiritualist church service while I was still a student
medium. I don't remember the details (I usually
don't), but I knew the man had passed from something to do with his heart (I felt an increased heart
rate) and I smelled bread being toasted in the morning (the air had the quality of morning light). The man
appeared to be making breakfast with the person the
message was for.

After the church service, she told me the man was
a coworker who'd died from a heart attack the previ-

ous year. They worked the graveyard shift on an ambulance crew and often made breakfast together in the morning at the stationhouse.

Mediumship is a sacred communication between those in Spirit and their loved ones still on the physical plane. To confirm that a person is still alive—perhaps unseen, but still very much alive—and in a good place and to help someone find peace is a great gift.

Mediumship brings messages and guidance

Mediumship needs to have useful purpose in the life of the person receiving the message, or it's beside the point. It takes effort and energy for folks in Spirit to communicate with us—they're usually not doing it just to say "hi."

While it's lovely to know that your great aunt Matilda is hanging out with you, and it's possible that all you need to know that day is that you're not alone and that you're loved, there's usually something more there.

Most often, guides and loved ones will give information the person needs to know. Sometimes that includes information about their past or present—how a loved one died, for instance, if there was doubt, or why certain things happened during their relationship. Loved ones in Spirit can give answers to lingering questions about the past, as well as advice and information about the present and even the future. Information about the past can bring solace and closure and help people find resolution.

These messages are meant to help you move forward in your life and keep your feet firmly planted on the path for your highest good. They won't give you the winning lottery numbers.

However, mediumship can do even more than that.

Mediumship connects you to your divine self

Mediumship doesn't just connect you with your late husband and help you figure out what to do with his ashes and provide you consolation that he continues on, although those are definitely meaningful and important things. It also connects you with Spirit and propels you further along your path, helping you grow and step into your authentic, powerful self.

Intuitive mediumship provides guidance for your highest path. It connects you with your own higher, inner, divine self and that of your loved ones and guides. This connection strengthens your experience and knowledge of Spirit, with the energy that connects all life.

The knowledge and information you can receive during your mediumship practice about the inner workings of life is invaluable. It helps you understand your role in this universe and how you are connected to everything else. It helps you find clarity and understanding on your path—past, present and future.

Benefits of developing your intuitive mediumship skills

Just because you have intuitive mediumship abilities doesn't mean you have to develop them or do anything with them in this lifetime. You're not required to. You have free will.

However, if you're still reading, you're probably interested in opening up, learning to control or fine tuning your intuitive and mediumship abilities. Here are some of the reasons why you might want to and benefits for doing so:

- **Connecting with your loved ones in Spirit—** knowing your own friends and family who have

passed on from this life are still with you and sup-
porting you can bring you tremendous peace.
Plus, folks in Spirit have been known to help you
through tricky things in this physical life. It's good
to have people on your side (especially if they're
invisible spirit ninjas).

- **Connecting with your spirit guides and your
  higher guidance**—there are plenty of people
  who like to give advice, but don't you want your
  advice to come from the highest source, one that
  truly has your highest and best good as its intent?
  Information from your divine self and your guides
  is of the highest quality and can be trusted to steer
  you correctly.

- **Feeling in tune with the universe**—life has its
  ups and downs because, well, it's life. Connecting
  with your intuition helps you weather the storms
  and sail more easily into calm and clear waters.
  The more you expand your awareness of how this
  universe works, the more you feel at home in it
  and able to navigate your way through life. Mediumship is an excellent way to access useful and
  important information about yourself, your path
  and your next steps.

• **Knowing how to shut it off**—being aware of things that other people aren't can make life tricky, especially if it feels out of control. No one wants to see or hear "dead people" when they're not ready for it. If your abilities feel out of control, if you're already receiving communication from Spirit and it doesn't always feel pleasant, developing your abilities will actually help you. Even if all you want to do is learn how to make it stop.

Chapter 3:
Set yourself up for success

The attitude and intent with which you start something sets the tone for how that experience is likely to unfold. How can you prepare yourself to successfully develop your intuitive mediumship abilities?

Here are a number of ways you can set yourself up for success.

Know your intent

Get clear on why you want to learn mediumship. Ask yourself about your motivations.

Are you serious or are you just playing around? Are you looking for fame and fortune? Or do you want to dabble just enough so you can spook yourself and your friends?

Dabbling, spooking and fame-seeking aren't good reasons to develop mediumship abilities. While fame and fortune might happen, it's not the reason to go into something. And spooking people—yourself or others—isn't the fun it's cracked up to be.

Good reasons to develop your abilities are going to be aligned with the benefits of mediumship. They include a desire to gain clarity into life after death, to find upliftment for yourself and others, and to bring healing to people going through the grief of losing a loved one. You might also seek unfoldment so that you learn how to safely and successfully develop the latent or uncontrolled gifts you know you have but don't yet understand.

Wanting to further understand mediumship so you that feel more sane and in control of your life is also a fine reason.

Set your expectations

Have high goals, but realistic expectations. Unfolding slowly and deliberately is healthier—and easier—than opening up all at once. Patience and persistence are essential.

It's also important to be practical and use common sense. Different people learn differently, at different rates and in different ways. Recognize that you're unique and, as such, your path isn't going to be quite the same as anyone else's. But many paths lead to the same destination. You'll get there if you keep at it.

Learn to set boundaries

I'll go into boundary setting in terms of mediumship later on, but boundaries are important in all aspects of your life. You need to learn to set boundaries in your everyday life and with the people around you, as well as with Spirit.

Start practicing now. Learn to say "no" if that's what your inner guidance (your intuition) tells you. Know what kinds of relationships you want to have and start moving forward into those—in terms of the emotions and behaviors you're willing to accept and receive from the people around you.

Find a class, church or mentor

The best way to develop and unfold mediumship skills is in a safe, loving, supportive environment.

Finding a class in a Spiritualist church taught by a qualified medium is an excellent option. Home circles can also be helpful for people who study better in a less formal environment.

41

If you don't have either of these options available where you live, look for a mentor. Mentoring can be done in-person or online. Finding someone to guide you through the process of unfolding is invaluable.

Whether you find a church or spiritual center, a home circle or a mentor, trust your intuition—in finding it in the first place and whether or not it feels like a good fit for you.

Create space in your life for your development

Even if you don't have a regular class or development circle, set aside consistent time in which you meditate and practice opening to Spirit. This creates a dependable routine in your own life, allowing you to more easily get in sync and into the energy needed to connect with Spirit.

It also lets your guides and teachers in Spirit know that you're serious and when they can get in touch with you—it establishes boundaries. If folks in Spirit know you're available Tuesday afternoons at 2 p.m., then they can leave you alone the rest of the week because they know when you'll be open and receptive.

Take care of yourself

Mediumship can sometimes be taxing on the body, mind and emotions. When you give readings to others, people receiving those readings often want a lot—they're usually in a difficult place in their life when they seek you out or when you're drawn to them. And mediums, by their nature, are sensitive to people's emotions and vibrations.

People who receive messages want confirmation, answers and healing. That, combined with the effort of attuning to Spirit, listening very closely and concentrating on the Spirit entities that are coming through so as to correctly understand and interpret their messages, can take a lot of energy when you're not used to it.

As you become more accustomed to using these abilities, it does get easier. Your intuitive muscles grow as you use them. And, as you learn how to deal with people's expectations and reactions when they receive readings, you learn how to be empathetic but detached enough not to take on other people's emotional stuff.

You need to take care of your mental and physical health. Eat well, exercise and maintain good company so you can stay positive and balanced. Taking care of yourself isn't selfish and optional. Self-care is vital and necessary.

Stay grounded, humble and in integrity

As you begin to develop your abilities, make sure you stay grounded. Remember that messages are from Spirit, not from you. They pass through you—you're the medium through which they pass.

Do your best to stay on a path of integrity. Don't let your desire for approval sway you. And don't let the approval and positive feedback from others (even though it's wonderful to know you're bringing through real, evidential information) go to your head. Stay humble. Keep learning. Remain connected to your divine self.

Use your power for good.

Chapter 4: Beginning your development

You can develop your intuitive mediumship abilities safely and with ease. This doesn't have to be a difficult, uncomfortable journey, and you don't need to be afraid. In fact, if you are feeling discomfort, that means you need to look at what you're doing, the way you're doing it and ask what it is that your intuition is trying to tell you. (And remember, while discomfort sometimes means to change what you're doing or how you're doing it, sometimes it's a feeling of being out of your comfort zone and indicates you're in a place of growth.)

I'm going to share the most important things I learned early on in my mediumship journey. They are what made the difference for me in knowing I could safely open up to Spirit, on my terms and in a way that felt good and comfortable to me. These will help you whether folks in Spirit are waking you up every night at 3 a.m. or whether you just have an inkling that they're there, but you don't know how to connect.

Learn to ground yourself

Grounding connects your energy to the natural energy field of the Earth. When you don't feel grounded, you can feel spacey, dizzy, off-balance, shaky, dazed, or things may seem unreal. When you're grounded, you live in the present moment.

You can intuitively tell if someone is grounded or not—and if they're not, you might call them ditzy, head-in-the-clouds, air-headed. Grounded people are connected with reality.

Grounding anchors you in the physical world in which you live, while allowing you to safely travel and experience the spiritual and astral worlds. It also helps you get rid of energy that isn't yours and that can be harmful to you if you take it in as your own energy. This happens to a lot of empathic folks.

Learning how to ground yourself is of vital importance as you develop your abilities and learn to get them under control. It'll help you feel calmer, less anxious and more confident as you walk your path.

Grounding exercises

Here are two grounding exercises I like to do. Both are quick—they should take only a minute or two each, so give them a try.

Lock into the Earth

Place your feet on the ground and sit tall in your seat, with your back straight and your sitting bones making contact with the seat. You can also do this standing up.

Visualize your crown extending to the sky and roots growing from the soles of your feet and penetrating deep into the earth.

Position your feet at a 45 degree angle outward, with your knees and legs opening outward from your hips. Visualize a key or knob on the soles of your feet. I think of bicycle shoes that lock into your bike pedals.

Now swivel your feet so they're parallel to each other while imagining they're locking into the Earth, connecting and grounding you. You can do this with or without shoes on, it doesn't matter.

You can even do it just with the intent that you are grounding down, but the small motion can make it seem more real and sets your intention.

Connected by light

Sitting or standing tall, visualize white light entering the crown of your head and traveling down your chakras, lighting and energizing each one in turn.

First your third eye becomes a brilliant purple, then your throat becomes bright blue, your heart turns an emerald green, your solar plexus radiates bright yellow, your navel glows orange and your root chakra burns a deep red.

From your root chakra, see a golden rope of light connecting you to the Earth. You are grounded and connected to the energy of all that is, to Infinite Intelligence.

Becoming more grounded on a daily basis

The more you incorporate the methods below into your everyday life, the easier it is to feel and stay grounded. These methods may look suspiciously like ways to take good care of your mental, physical and emotional health. They are. And they're what you need to do to successfully unfold your abilities.

Breathe

Spend a few minutes a day (even 2-3 minutes makes a difference) breathing deeply, all the way deep into your belly. Inhale. Exhale. Slow and easy.

If you feel like you don't have time even for that, try this: take a deep breathe all the way into your belly. Hold it for 1 or 2 seconds. Let it out through your mouth with an "aaahhh." Do that 2 more times. There, you're done.

You've come into the present moment, even just for a few breaths and grounded yourself. You can do this any time you feel stressed or distracted.

Spend time in nature

Whatever element of nature you most connect with—the woods, the ocean, the desert, the mountains—spend time there. I often recommend people go for walks in the woods and connect with the energy of the trees. Trees are deeply rooted in the earth and reach up toward the sky, affording them an excellent flow of energy and grounding.

Take Epsom salt baths

Add about a cup of Epsom salts (you can also use sea salt, Hawaiian salt or Himalayan salt) to your bath water and relax, letting the water soothe away your flighty energy and connect you to the present. If you can't take a bath, or don't like them, use a salt scrub in the shower.

Exercise

Connecting with your physical body through whatever exercise you choose is grounding. It makes you pay attention to what's going on in the here and now, plus it has all sorts of emotional, physiological and mental benefits. It doesn't matter what the exercise is, as long as it uses your body—walking, yoga, running, kayaking, bicycling, whatever you like. You can combine exercise with active meditation, which you can read about in chapter 5.

Eat well

Eat real foods that come from ingredients you can recognize (whole foods). Remove processed foods from your diet.

Nourishing your body is extremely important in living a grounded, well-balanced life. Some people advise eating root vegetables, as they come from the Earth. Others say that meat is very grounding, but that you shouldn't eat it before meditation, mediumship or healing work.

I say: figure out what works for you and do that. I happen to need a fair amount of protein in my diet, which I'm not good at getting from a vegetarian diet. However, I don't like to eat a lot of meat. And I try not to eat too many carbs. Which means I get to eat a lot of veggies, plus some meat or fish, plus some carbs. And occasionally dessert.

It's like the Michael Pollan quote, "Eat food. Mostly plants. Not too much."

You don't have to be perfect at this. And you don't need to diet. But you can make improvements over time.

Use crystals and stones

Dense, hard minerals help to ground and transmit energy. Hematite is an excellent grounding stone. It's made of iron oxide and used to provide protection, to stimulate the mind and to ground out energy. Varieties of hematite include magnetite, specularite and iron rose.

Other grounding stones are blue or black kyanite, black tourmaline and obsidian.

Setting your intention: asking for your highest and best good

Now that you're grounded and know what steps to take to live a healthy life, it's time to learn how to set your intention. Learning that I had control over what I experienced when I connected with Spirit made all the difference in my confidence and willingness to be open to communication from folks in Spirit.

When students first become interested in mediumship, they're often concerned about connecting with beings that are frightening or spooky. Given how ghosts and death are often portrayed in our culture, that's not surprising. But it doesn't have to be this way. And, actually, it shouldn't be a scary experience at all. There doesn't need to be anything dark, negative or remotely terrifying about mediumship.

It all depends on your intent.

If you ask for your highest and best good as you open up to Spirit, that's all you'll get. This goes back to the laws of attraction and continuity, two of the natural laws that govern mediumship. You attract to you what you want and ask for—both in the physical and nonphysical worlds.

So what should you ask for, exactly? What are the boundaries you should set?

I state it simply as, "I ask only for my highest and best good."

As I state my intent, I'm also setting my boundaries—my highest good is all I will accept and nothing else.

This seems almost too simple, but it's not. My intent is everything. And it comes from a solid foundation of everyday boundary setting.

Is it redundant to ask for my highest AND best good? Aren't they the same thing? They probably are. In my case, it's habit, because it's what I was taught and I've said it so long (mentally and aloud) that I just keep saying it. You say what works for you. "I ask only for my highest good," is probably sufficient. And then know that's all you'll get.

Setting and maintaining your boundaries

Setting intent and asking only for your highest good is closely related to setting your boundaries. Learning to set boundaries is incredibly important in all aspects of your life and relationships. But especially so as you open to Spirit energy.

You want to make sure the experiences you have with spirit guides and folks on the other side of life are positive ones that leave you feeling good and uplifted. Working with Spirit isn't supposed to feel creepy. Setting your intent and having solid boundaries ensures that it's a good experience.

Everyday boundaries

You set boundaries and determine how you allow people to treat you in your everyday life all the time, often without thinking about it. Partly, you do this by how you treat others. If you're often angry and short-tempered with others, you're likely to receive similar treatment in your dealings with people, especially those close to you. The Golden Rule—treat others as you'd like them to treat you—has existed throughout the centuries in various faiths and philosophies for a reason.

However, if you're respectful and kind during the majority of your days, not only are the people around you more likely to treat you respectfully and with kindness, but you come from a much firmer foundation when you ask and expect respect, love and kindness in return. And when others aren't treating you in a manner you're OK with, it's easier to set firm, loving boundaries and behavioral expectations.

It can be hard to change ingrained patterns of behavior and it's not something that happens overnight. Yet, with time and self-awareness, it can happen.

Setting boundaries with Spirit

If all you want to receive from opening to Spirit and your higher/inner self is goodness and love, then that's what you need to ask for.

It's a similar interaction as when I'm having a conversation with someone. I know that, in my daily life, I want to have positive interactions with people which leave me feeling generally good about myself and the world around me.

In order to have good interactions, I stay aware of my emotional state, my posture and body language, and the words and tone of voice I use. I breathe. I smile. I give people the benefit of the doubt. I know we're each doing the best we can in any given moment.

At this point in my life, people rarely yell at me or say hurtful things. My boundaries are set firmly that this sort of experience is something I don't invite or accept. If, during an odd occurrence (because it takes all sorts of people to make up this world, plus I have kids), someone does react to me in an angry, hurtful or otherwise unpleasant way, I do my best to stay calm and pay attention to my emotions, breathing, body language, tone, etc., and let them know how I wish to be treated and when they've stepped over the line in their interaction with me.

Sometimes I have the presence of mind to calmly state my boundaries. "Please speak calmly and politely."

Other times I remove myself from the situation. "I'm going to go now." "We can talk about this later." "Mummy needs a timeout."

You can do the same with Spirit—whether you're feeling the energy of the world around you, channeling an excarnate energy, or acting as a conduit for mediumship messages from those on the other side of life. If it feels uncomfortable or unpleasant, ask Spirit to take the emotions that aren't yours (then release them) or ask the folks in Spirit to step back to a comfortable level.

You get to set the boundaries. You can say, "No."

What's great is that this works even better in your work with Spirit than it does in the physical world.

If there's an angry person shouting at me, I can ask them to stop and let them know how they are acting is not OK with me. They may or may not respond to me in the way I'd like.

With folks in Spirit, you can ask them to step back and they have to comply with your desire and intent. There is no need for negotiation, as long as you're able to set and keep firm boundaries. When it comes to energy, your word (or thought) is law.

The best way to do this is to believe you can. And to practice it in your everyday, physical life.

Just like exercising makes your muscles stronger and enables you to go further, faster, flexing your spiritual and energetic muscles helps them grow as well.

Boring stuff, I know. Much of living a good, metaphysical life is about taking care of your physical life and living it the best way you can.

So the next time someone in your everyday life tests your boundaries, open your heart, set your limits and enforce them, asking only for your highest good. And know that you're improving not only your daily life, but your spiritual one, too.

Chapter 5: Meditation

Meditation is a wonderful thing. But it's like exercise—you don't realize how much you enjoy it and how much your body and mind need it until you start doing it regularly. And it can be hard to get over the initial hump of getting into a routine.

And, like exercise, or any of the other things that you know are good for you but still don't want to do, the decision to meditate regularly and the motivation to do it has to come from within you. I can make a persuasive case for meditation, which I'll attempt to do below, but unless you decide it's a good idea and are willing to put in the effort, all my arguments are pointless.

So I'm going to proceed with the understanding you've already decided that including meditative time in your daily life is a good idea. But maybe you don't know quite how to go about it. Or you're still looking at meditation with old eyes and think it's something more mystical and achievable than it really is. And how does meditation help with mediumship?

The benefits of meditation

Regular meditation can do wonderful things for your life, in all areas of your experience.

Physical and psychological benefits of meditation include: reduced anxiety, lowered blood pressure, improved mood, better memory, better immune response, and being able to release ways of thinking that don't serve you well.

Spiritual and emotional benefits include getting to know yourself better, connecting with your divine self and your guides, understanding what you're doing here on this Earth, and healing old wounds, to name a few. You may find your outlook on life changing as you drop old perceptions and beliefs and take on ones of higher vibration. You may learn to treat others as you'd like them to treat you. And you may learn to look upwards, move forward and experience the joy and love of being connected to Infinite Intelligence and to your divine self.

Chapter 5: Meditation

When you're working on developing intuitive and mediumship skills, meditation allows you connect with your higher self and receive guidance and wisdom. It opens you up to your highest good while teaching you how to focus your mind and connect with specific frequencies of energy (which is what you do when you connect with folks in Spirit).

It also helps you heal old stuff.

Going within and learning about the self in all its aspects brings a true and deep knowledge of your motivations, emotions, thinking patterns—how and why you do the things you do. You become aware of yourself on all levels—physical, mental and spiritual—and learn to love, accept and forgive many things about yourself.

When you are physically self-aware, you know not only your limitations, but your body's capabilities and your potential as well. The same is true for your mental and spiritual self. And once you know yourself, you can come to like and accept yourself. Being able to realize and accept your past mistakes enables you to let them go and move forward in your evolution.

When I meditate regularly, I feel more energized, I start my days with a better attitude and feel aligned with the universe. I struggle less. New opportunities arise with ease and I cease to have the desire to obsessively play Candy Crush and check social media.

Why does this happen? When I connect with Spirit, my source, I raise my vibration to be in sync with the highest good for my life and that allows me to step into the flow of co-creation. Basically, I stop thinking so much, I get out of my own way and allow goodness into my life. I quit struggling.

You live in a world with so much external input—there's so much coming at you all of the time from so many sources. Meditation gives you a break from the overwhelming emotional and sensory overload of life. It allows you to reset, connect in with your inner self and find peace and clarity. Or it will, if you do it enough.

Ways to meditate

There's even more good news about meditation—there are many ways to do it. Some are methods that may not first come to mind when you think about how to include meditation in your life.

Chapter 5: Meditation

What do you think of when you think of meditation? Possibly a person sitting crossed legged with their hands resting palms up on their knees, thumb and forefinger making a circle. They sit, straight but relaxed, a look of serenity and enlightenment on their face as their conscious mind lets go and floats in the heavens with the angels, gods and wise ones.

That's one way to do it. And it is the style of meditation that, as a developing intuitive medium, you'll probably end up moving toward (specific hand postures and looks of enlightenment not required). But if you haven't mediated much up until this point, it's not necessarily the place you need to start.

First, I'm going to cover some meditation techniques to help you learn to get into a meditative state. Then I'll tell you about some additional ways you can meditate that you may not have thought of before.

When you start meditating, one of the most important things for you to know is that your meditation is a success any time you sit down, close your eyes and breathe. The attempt, in and of itself is a success. What happens when you do it is secondary, especially in the beginning.

Yes, hopefully your meditation leaves you feeling more relaxed and centered than when you began. But relaxing can feel like hard work sometimes. Don't get hung up on the outcome. And don't expect yourself to be able to just close your eyes and breathe once or twice and be transported to nirvana. Your brain will likely continue to whir and churn and remind you of all the things you've forgotten to do. I still have days where that's how my meditation goes. It's OK. Plus it can be useful to remember the thing I've forgotten for the past 2 weeks.

These methods are helpful if you want to find moments of mental stillness during meditation but have difficulty with your mind constantly wandering away or feeling anxious. I like to think of them as giving your brain something to do so that it can let go of all the other stuff it likes to pay attention to and hold on to. This allows your intuition and wise mind to step in.

Inhale, exhale

Meditation is really all about breathing. Breathing in. Breathing out. Paying attention to that breath—and, by doing so, distracting your brain from all the other things it usually thinks about.

As you inhale, mentally say to yourself, *inhale.*

As you exhale, mentally say to yourself, *exhale.*

Repeat.

If that doesn't seem like enough to focus your mind, try saying to yourself: *Now I am inhaling. Now I am exhaling.* It takes a little longer to say these phrases in your mind, hopefully taking up most of the space of your inhale and exhale, and keeping your mind more focused.

I also like the humor I find in it. *Now I am inhaling.* How much more in the present moment can you be than when you are thinking to yourself about the very thing you are doing to keep your body alive?

Counting

Counting sheep is a widely-known method for falling asleep (at least you've probably heard of it, even if you haven't tried it). Counting helps you concentrate and focus your mind on something, which allows it to relax.

There are a couple of methods of counting that I like to use.

Counting to 10

As you inhale, mentally count *1*.

As you exhale, mentally count *2*.

Continue going: inhale *3*, exhale *4*, inhale *5*, exhale *6*, inhale *7*, exhale *8*, inhale *9*, exhale*10*.

Then start again from 1 and repeat.

Counting each in breath and out breath

As you inhale, slowly count *1, 2, 3, 4* in your mind, for the length of your inhalation.

As you exhale, slowly count *1, 2, 3, 4, 5* in your mind, for the length of your exhalation.

It's best if you can make your exhale 1 count longer than your inhale.

Or, if you enjoy counting the beats of music, you can inhale for *1, 2, 3, 4* and exhale for *5, 6, 7, 8*, with a count of rest at the end.

Mindfulness

Mindfulness meditation falls along the lines of what you probably traditionally think of as meditation, although, with practice, it can be done pretty much anywhere, not just alone in a quiet place.

The goal of mindfulness meditation is to help you focus on the present and live in each present moment. It does this by helping you focus on your breath. By becoming more present with yourself, as you are right now, you're able to participate more fully in each moment of your life. It can also help you learn to focus your mind as you gently bring it back (over and over and over again) to the present moment each time it wanders off.

An important thing to know about mindfulness meditation is that its goal isn't to stop thinking or to be able to sit with an empty mind. Its point is for you to learn to notice what is at the focus of your attention and to be able to move that point of focus, without judgement, to what you want it to be (in this case, your breath). Mindfulness is about accepting yourself where you are in each present moment.

Within mindfulness meditation, there is a range of techniques. You can meditate with your eyes open or closed, for instance. Try out different things and find out what works best for you (I like to close my eyes).

A mindfulness meditation technique

- As you sit, breathe in and out, deeply and gently.
- Take three deep breaths.
- Allow yourself to breath normally. Don't force your breath. Notice your breath.

- Notice how your breath enters your body and how it leaves it.

- Notice how your breath feels at the first moment of your inhalation, at the fullness of your inhalation, at the first moment of your exhalation and at the end of your exhale. Pay attention to the edges of your breath at the moments it enters and leaves your body.

- As your mind wanders, gently bring it back to your body and your breath.

- As thoughts continue to come into your mind (which they will do, it's just the way of thoughts), bring your attention back to your breath. Release any judgement you have of yourself for having thoughts. They're OK and natural. Just notice, without judgement, that you've been thinking and move your attention back to your breath.

- Each time a thought comes up, you can say/think to yourself "thought" then go back to paying attention to your breath.

You can practice this mindfulness meditation for 1 minute or for 30 minutes, it's up to you. And there are lots of other mindfulness techniques, this is just one of them.

Mindful eating

Mindful eating also brings you into the present moment and focuses not only your mind but your taste buds.

You can do this exercise with specific foods (chocolate is usually a favorite) or during your every-day meals.

Slowly take a bite of your food. Hold it in your mouth for a moment and allow your mouth to experience its flavors and texture. What do you smell? How does it feel on your tongue? Is it warm or cold?

Go into the experience and allow yourself to become immersed in it.

Chew and swallow slowly. Feel the food go down your throat. Does it nourish you? How does your body react to it?

Try this exercise the next time you eat or drink something. When you take your first sip of your morning coffee or tea, connect with the moment and sink into it. Really feel and taste what's happening. This is mindfulness.

This is also an extremely useful exercise in developing your intuitive senses of taste and smell.

Mindful listening

Close your eyes, breathe deeply and listen. What do you hear? In this present moment, what sounds are around you? How far away can you hear? Can you locate where sounds are coming from—in front or behind you, to your left or right?

Another way to develop mindful listening is to have someone ring a bell or sound a chime in a quiet room and listen for the very edges of the sound—the moment at which you can no longer hear the sound vibrations in the air.

This technique brings you into the present moment, which is where you're able to access your intuition and deeper wisdom. It also helps to develop your intuitive sense of hearing.

Guided meditation

There are many types of guided meditations and uses for them. Guided meditations can be done using a recording or a meditation leader reading a guided meditation script. They often make use of visualizations that enable you to accomplish something useful.

Listening to a voice guide you through a series of visualizations or mental actions gives your mind something to focus on and can keep it from wandering off. Some people love guided meditations and find they're able to achieve deeper and more profound meditative experiences. Other people find it annoying or distracting to have someone telling them what to do.

I've found that even if you find your visualization going somewhere other than where your guide is leading you, guided meditations can be a great starting off point. It's OK to follow your intuition and see what you need to see during your meditation, even if it isn't quite the same as how you're being led.

Some examples of guided meditations include:

- Meeting your spirit guides (see chapter 9)
- Chakra opening (for cleansing or healing)
- Increasing psychic abilities by opening specific chakras (to increase clairvoyance, for instance)
- Loving-kindness meditations for yourself and others (see chapter 6)
- Relaxation, anxiety-reduction
- Healing

Other ways to meditate

Sitting quietly isn't the only way to meditate. You can meditate while using your body, too.

For some people, that's through a regular yoga or Tai Chi practice. Or even walking while allowing your thoughts to deepen and wander. (Walking is a great way to access your intuition.) This is called *physical meditation*.

For others, they find a meditative state while doing repetitive tasks, like folding laundry, vacuuming or showering. Or coloring. It allows you to get into a relaxed state of mind where enough of your brain is focused on the task at hand that you let go of all the other things you usually think about. This is called *active meditation*.

Physical meditation

When people focus on their spiritual lives they often seek to get out of their bodies. Your body can be uncomfortable and annoying, after all. But your body is the very thing you use to experience life in this form, on this planet, in this current time. It's not only OK to live fully present in your body (as it is right now), it's imperative that you do. Distracting yourself from your body won't solve the issues you have with it

Physical mediation carries with it the benefit of improving your physical health at the same time you reap the mental, emotional and spiritual rewards of meditation. And that, in turn, makes it easier to live with the body that you have.

During physical meditation, you become aware of your body and, by focusing exclusively on it, you can eliminate the constant chatter from your mind. This creates stillness which allows the space and quiet for wisdom to enter. This type of meditation makes use of the breath, encouraging long, slow breaths as you breathe in life's vital energy while performing a series of movements meant to strengthen and invigorate your body.

Examples of physical meditation are yoga, Tai Chi and even walking or running.

Yoga meditation

In a yoga practice, for instance, awareness of your body and breath are fundamental pillars of performing asanas. You are supposed to be fully present in your body. The effect of this focus allows you to release the constant thoughts that go through your mind—what you're going to cook for dinner, who you need to call back, what needs to go on the grocery list, what bill you need to pay, what you should do about that tricky relationship, and on and on. By giving your attention instead to your body, breath, posture and gaze, you gain all the benefits of meditation. Plus, you're getting the physical benefits of doing yoga.

Walking meditation

Walking and meditation go together so well you may find yourself already doing it without even meaning to. It can be done as a form of mindfulness—of being aware and in the present moment. One foot in front of the other. It can be used as a way to open up and connect with your intuition—allowing your feet to take you wherever they want to go. Walking meditation can also be used in conjunction with a mantra. (See chapter 7 for an intuitive walking exercise.)

If you have trouble sitting still, walking meditation may be the very thing you need.

Here's a simple walking meditation:

- Go outside—outside of your house in the suburbs, somewhere in the woods, in middle of a city or at a nearby playground. It really doesn't matter where you go.

- Stand still for a moment.

- Notice your body. How does it feel? Notice any areas that are stiff or aching, as well as areas that feel good and energized, or simply that feel a lack of pain.

- Notice the air around you on your skin. Is it cool or warm? Is there a breeze? Can you smell anything in the air?

- Take just a moment to connect with the Earth beneath your feet and inhale fully and exhale.

- Begin walking. Move your awareness to the muscles in your legs, feet, abs, hips and pelvis as you move. Keep walking, mindfully, letting the alternating steps of your right and left feet become a meditative rhythm.

- Feel the soles of your feet in your shoes as they make contact with the ground. Be aware of your arms swinging as you walk. Let them go where they naturally want to go.

- As your mind wanders, bring it back to the rhythm of your walk. Left foot, right foot. Breath in, breath out.

- Continue walking, bringing your attention back to your breath and your body as many times as you need to.
- When you're ready to stop, stop. Stand still and breathe, noticing how your body feels now that it's no longer in motion.

Active meditation

In active meditation, also known as action and meditation, you incorporate a physical skill into your meditation. Concentrating on a task stills your mind, allows it to focus and releases your constant stream of thoughts. Plus you get really good at doing the thing you're focusing on.

You can incorporate this type of meditation into everyday crafts such as knitting, crocheting, coloring, spinning yarn or flower arranging. You can also meditate while washing the dishes, vacuuming the house, weeding, mowing the lawn or folding laundry.

Folding laundry meditation

The next time you're staring down the laundry pile, reach in and pick up an item to fold. Don't worry which item you should fold next. Don't think about how much there is to do, or if you need to put the next load in the dryer, or if it's time to get the kids ready for bed or whatever else is on your usual mental to-do list.

Look at the item you're folding. Feel the texture of the fabric against your skin. Note the edges of the item, how it's made, its seams and craftsmanship. Fold it deliberately, carefully. Notice the breath going in and out of your body, and how your hands and arms work together to complete the task. Put it down and pick up the next item. There, you meditated and folded laundry at the same time.

Coloring meditation

Do you remember coloring as a kid? I have vivid and fond memories of hours spent with my mother over a Beatrix Potter coloring book. We'd choose a page and work on it together, choosing colors and conferring as we filled in images of Peter Rabbit. I was probably about 6 years old at the time. Beyond quality time spent with a loved one, the emotion the memory has left with me is one of peace and calm.

That's because coloring is a way to get into a meditative state. As you choose each color and fill in sections of the image, your mind focuses and stills.

Even if you start out busy and distracted, determined to just get the page colored already, you'll eventually calm down and release your stress and anxiety as you go through the soothing motions of coloring shapes and choosing new colors. You can't do it wrong. Even if you go outside the lines.

You can access your intuition through coloring meditation. But even if nothing else, you'll calm your mind.

Meditation in everyday life

You can bring meditation and mindfulness to everyday aspects of your life. Whether you're doing yoga or the dishes, or walking from your car to the store, you can become aware of your breath and focus on the activity you're doing. Become present in the moment, in your body. Release thoughts of judgement and worry. When you have them, notice them and let them go.

You can do this in so many everyday moments of your life—give it a try and see.

Making the effort and taking the time to meditate daily—however you manage to do it—is truly a gift you give to yourself. It's easy to say you don't have time or can't make time (and it probably makes you anxious just thinking about it). But once you get over your initial resistance and start, you'll see how vital a part of your life meditation becomes. The benefits are worth the effort.

Regular meditation will help you learn to focus your mind and let go of churning thoughts. It will teach you that you are not your thoughts, but can instead be a non-judgmental observer of them. This helps immensely in developing your mediumship abilities and is a vital step in doing so.

Keep in mind that developing mediumship abilities takes time. Often a lot of time. Don't expect to pop in a meditation CD once or twice and get immediate results or be able to be whisked off to magic meditation land where you confer with guides and discarnate entities.

If at first you're distracted, or you fall asleep, it's OK. Keep at it. Try a different style of meditating and see if that works better for you. You can't fail meditation, even if it doesn't seem like what you expected it to be. Remember that every meditation builds on the last and is never a waste of time.

Chapter 6:
Raise your vibration

Spiritualists often talk about "raising your vibration" as a necessary part of developing mediumship abilities. They are most often referring to the idea of raising your energetic frequency so that you can better connect with folks in Spirit, who are commonly thought of as being of a higher vibration and having to lower their vibration enough so that you can communicate with them.

I don't think it quite works that way, in terms of raising and lowering vibration. Communicating with Spirit and connecting with your intuition is more about being able to dial into specific frequencies. However, it definitely helps if you have a clear channel to do so—you get much less static and fewer crossed signals. Raising your vibration—clearing up your own energy—is the way to do that.

You've probably encountered people in your life who radiate peace and love. Their energy feels clear. They're grounded and seem to move through life with ease. You want to be around them. That's the person you're turning into. Just remember not to compare your insides with other people's outsides. They still have their issues and challenges, just as you will. But your way of facing them and dealing with them will change, due to the way the way you look at the world changes. That's a result of a change in your vibration.

As I explained in Chapter 1, everything in this universe vibrates. The frequency at which it vibrates governs how that energy manifests. While it's tempting to think of frequency and vibration solely in terms of higher and lower, it's a bit more nuanced than that. There's also the clarity of the frequency.

There's only so much raising of your vibration that you can do while you're living in a physical body. By the very nature of your existence on the Earth plane, you're going to have a certain vibration. But you can increase the clarity of your vibration.

There are entire religions and thought philosophies related to how you can live a life of clearer energy and intent, so it's hardly something that can be covered in a single chapter. However, there are some things that you can get started with.

Many of these methods and ideas are also ways you can ground yourself. It all goes hand in hand and is part of the continuum of energy between our physical and spiritual selves.

Accept responsibility for yourself and your life

Spiritualism teaches personal responsibility. As one of its principles states, "We make our own happiness or unhappiness as we obey or disobey Nature's physical and spiritual laws."

Personal responsibility means that your life is the way it is right now, in this moment, because of the thoughts, decisions and actions you've had over the course of your life and even in the time before it.

I believe that we choose the lives we live—in a time before we come into this life, we even choose the great challenges we experience during our lifetime. Why we choose to have some of the experiences we do does seem baffling, but there is a purpose to it. That doesn't make the people who hurt us absolved of wrongdoing or place blame upon us for the experiences we have. There's a difference between blame and responsibility.

Taking responsibility for your thoughts, your words and your actions and their outward manifestation creating the life you're living and will live doesn't assign blame; it gives you power. Because it means you can change what you're experiencing. You can change your vibration.

Be aware of your thoughts

You are not your thoughts. You have thoughts. And your thoughts help to create your reality. So learn to become more aware of them, without judgment. Notice them. Notice the direction they're taking you and how you feel as they do.

If you don't like how you feel as a result of what you're thinking, modify your thinking. Consider different possibilities and outcomes. Think about what you'd like to happen rather than what you fear might happen.

Learn about the common cognitive distortions our minds convince us of: catastrophizing, black and white thinking, overgeneralization, jumping to conclusions, blaming, shoulds, fallacies, etc. Know what direction your thoughts often go in—so that you can catch yourself and change direction. Mindfulness meditation is very helpful for this.

I tend to catastrophize, especially when it comes to my kids. If I'm not careful and being aware of what's going on in my head, one small thing can lead me down a spiraling path into bleakness where they either live at home until they're 40 or end up institutionalized. But because I know I do it, I can catch myself and either kindly encourage myself to think differently or laugh at my foibles.

Remember the part about not judging yourself. Be kind to yourself. And, if your mind keeps going places that feel too difficult or untamed, it's OK to seek professional mental health help and treatment.

Be aware of what you expose yourself to

We're constantly bombarded with information in one form or another—whether that's music, advertising, TV shows or movies. What are you letting into your consciousness?

Consider the types of TV shows or movies you like to watch. Are they uplifting? Or are they full of violence, gore or horror? That goes for the music you listen to and the books you read as well. What you expose yourself to affects you—how you think, how you feel, how you react to other people and the world.

If you have the TV or radio on all the time, turn it off. Allow yourself to rest in quiet. Stop watching or reading the news as much. Most news reports create fear and feed off your fear. It's OK to not know everything that's going on everywhere in the news—and it's actually impossible to know about everything happening in the world or even in your neighborhood. The good stuff is underreported. Look around your family, your life, and your surroundings and see what's going right instead.

One of the side effects of raising your vibration and working with Spirit is that violent entertainment will stop appealing to you. You won't want to watch horror movies (there's always an exception, but this is usually true). You won't enjoy music that's violent or hateful or even especially loud. This is because you'll be tuned into a different frequency and you won't want to muddy up your vibration with fear or anger, because it doesn't feel good.

Plus, as you open up to Spirit, you don't want that stuff in your consciousness. You don't want to be thinking about ghouls and murder. You want to raise your consciousness to something higher.

Take care of your body

You need your physical body. It's the vessel through which you experience life at the moment. No body = no physical life. So take care of it.

Great ways to take care of your body and raise your vibration are exercise and eating wholesome food.

Exercise does so much to clear out foggy thinking while grounding you and making you physically healthier. And it doesn't have to be crazy hard exercise. Walking, yoga, swimming, bike riding, dancing, gardening—anything that gets your body moving and your heart and lungs working to the best of your physical ability.

Exercises with forward movement, such as walking, are beneficial for you in many ways. There's something about walking that literally helps you move forward in life. If you feel stuck in any way in your life, go for a walk. It will, as my husband says, "get the stink blowed off you."

Your life is busy, but incorporating exercise into it will help you move through your days more easily. And it'll help you on an energetic level.

What you put into your body is also important. Your body is a machine. It needs good fuel to run. You don't run an engine that needs a certain quality of gasoline on something that's inferior and expect it to run, do you? You don't put kerosene in your car. So don't put inferior fuel in your body.

Your body is designed to run on real food—food that you can tell what it really was when it came out of the ground, not processed food substances. You don't need to go vegan. (I'm not. I can't even handle vegetarianism.) You don't even need to buy all organic food from your local farmer's market (although that's not a bad idea). But the fuel you put in your body matters.

Eating wholesome food raises your overall vibration—just like regular exercise increases your muscle mass which raises your basal metabolism.

Meditate

Not to sound like a song put on repeat, but meditation is vital if you're on a path of spiritual growth. It will help you access your inner self and wisdom. It will help you find that still, small spot of calm inside yourself. It's a great vibration raiser.

Meditation teaches you the skills to focus (and refocus) your mind that you'll need to connect with friends and loved ones in Spirit. It teaches you the skills you need to be able to discipline your mind and tune into the specific frequencies of different Spirit energies.

As I covered in the last chapter, there are many different meditation techniques. Find what works for you and start there. Ultimately, you'll want to be able to sit in meditation and consciously connect with Spirit in order to receive messages in a controlled manner. But, to start, remember that there's no failing in meditation. You can't meditate wrong.

Spend time in nature

Most of us live insular, sedentary lives. We spend our time largely indoors, often sitting at desks while practicing poor posture and experiencing overstimulation from screens and social media (I'm not technology bashing—I'm a geek at heart and love gadgets). This is just how our lives are set up in today's society and we often have to make a conscious effort to break out of these habits and modes of being.

Nature is good for you. It connects you to the Earth and the Earth's energy. It grounds you and cleans your energy. When you feel overwhelmed in life, go and hug a tree. Seriously. Trees are great grounding, clearing forces, with their roots deep in the Earth and their branches raising toward the sky. They know how to move energy. And, if you listen quietly, you can hear them talk. Our planet is an intelligent being and all her creatures can communicate in their own way and in their own language.

Whatever your favorite aspect of nature is—the forest, the beach, the mountains, the desert—go out of your way if necessary to spend time in it, especially when you're feeling low energetically or emotionally. It'll lift your spirits and raise your vibration.

Even taking a few moments to stop and observe nature can help. As you walk to your car in the morning or evening after work, look at the plants around you. Observe the trees, the bushes, the flowers. Even noticing the grass and other plants growing up through cracks in the sidewalk counts. I admire small flowers and other "weeds" growing in the cracks in the concrete, or tree roots raising up sidewalks and parking lot asphalt. Can you feel their tenacity and will to survive? Or the intricate, perfect beauty of how a flower forms or the leaves on the trees appear to turn over and show their undersides when it's going to rain?

You are a part of this natural world. Often, as humans, we hold ourselves apart from the world. We put a lot of effort into protecting ourselves from the world—with clothes, houses, cars. We want to stay warm and comfortable. And while there's nothing wrong with that, you need to connect and reconnect with nature to tap into who you truly are.

Heal your past

We've all got baggage. At least I know I do. There's no shame if you do as well. Life can be hard and rocky at times and you do the best you can with what you have and what you know in each moment.

If you've still got past hurts you haven't moved on from, I urge you to work on healing them. You may be limiting yourself with your thoughts of what you believe you deserve to experience in this life. These limiting beliefs affect all aspects of your life and development and are usually based on false beliefs and misunderstandings of what's really true.

If you've been abused, for instance, you may feel shame and unworthiness. You may feel that you're unlovable and that there's something innately wrong and ugly deep inside you—that if people ever saw into the "real" you, they'd flee in horror. However, this is not the truth of who you are. You believe these things about yourself because of the abuse you've experienced. You were taught to believe these lies so you wouldn't reveal the truth of your abuse and they are the false foundation upon which you've built your understanding of yourself. It's OK. You did the best you could at the time. You're not at fault. You are, however, now responsible for yourself and your life and are being called to heal these wounds. Your inner self wants these issues to be worked on and cleared up. Your divine self wants you to release what no longer serves you.

There are many ways to heal your past—contemplation, journaling, spiritual healing and counseling are just a few. Mental health therapy or counseling can be a vital resource and there's no shame in seeing a counselor or therapist to help you work through past experiences which are affecting your life.

Earlier I talked about how we choose to have the experiences we do in this lifetime. I do believe this is true—at least for me. You're welcome to come to your own understanding. When the question of "why" comes up: Why did these things happen to me? Why did I choose the horrible experiences I went through that still affect me today? (I'm still working on my own healing; we're all works in progress.) The conclusion I come to is that I wanted to learn compassion and how to forgive myself and others. I wanted to be able to relate to others in pain and turmoil. I wanted the challenge of starting from a place of difficulty and low vibration and moving toward one of clarity, understanding and a clear, high vibration.

I don't know what your journey has been, nor what you are here on this Earth to experience and learn. And I won't presume to speak for you. What I do know is that the call to walk a spiritual path is a call to growth and healing. And you're capable of so much more than you realize.

Practice forgiveness and compassion

Forgiveness is a necessary skill to learn in this life. From small slights to huge betrayals and abuses, life tends to give us plenty of instances to learn and practice forgiveness.

Practicing forgiveness can be hard. When it comes to forgiving others, you may feel that they don't deserve to be forgiven (and perhaps rightly so). But forgiveness isn't about doing something for the person who harmed you. Forgiveness is a gift you give to yourself.

Forgiveness allows you to let go of the emotional weight of what you've been holding onto. It can be hard work, but it's ultimately a relief.

Forgiveness work is a lot like grieving—you go through stages and you often repeat some of them several times. It's a process. There are people in my life who I have gone through the process of forgiving several times and in different ways and I'm still not quite done yet. Some hurts go deep, down to your foundation.

There are a number of ways to go about forgiving the people in your past for their transgressions. Here are some that work for me. Take and use what works for you. Also, keep in mind that sometimes the person you most need to forgive and have compassion for is yourself, for the role you played (or think you played) in the situations and circumstances you're still holding onto.

Walking forgiveness meditation

I love walking meditations—whether I set out with a problem in mind that I allow my brain and higher self to work out while I walk, or I use a mantra, or do some mindful walking or I just want to clear my head. Walking works well for me.

If I want to work on forgiveness (and sometimes I don't know this at the start of the walk, but it's what comes up during the course of it), I think of that person as I walk and, to the rhythm of my own steps, I say, "I forgive you, I forgive you, I forgive you." I do this until the energy of forgiveness starts to flow. Sometimes I say this mentally, in my head. Other times, I feel the need to say it out loud. You can whisper it or you can shout it, whatever you feel you need to do to get the energy moving.

When you first say, "I forgive you," it may feel like a lie. The energy that goes with those words may feel like it's crunchy and grinding against itself. You may feel a lot of resistance. That's OK. Keep walking and keep saying it until that feeling of resistance softens and loosens up, like a clenched muscle that you're slowly relaxing and stretching. You don't need to force it—let it go at its own pace, give it the space and the breath it needs. Keep breathing. If you feel over-whelmed, breathe deeply. Allow your lungs to expand and fill. Then, as you exhale, allow more forgiveness to flow out from you.

If you get to the point of feeling the energy within you flow unrestricted as you say your mantra of "I forgive you," then either finish your walk or move onto another person for whom you are still holding feelings of resentment or hurt.

If you don't get to that point, it's OK. You can take a lot of walks. You may also find that you feel like you've forgiven them, but then something comes up later (that day, the next year, whenever) and you realize you still have more forgiveness work to do. That's totally normal. Keep at it.

Loving kindness meditation

One of the things I really like about loving kind-ness meditation is its practice of compassion. You need compassion—for others and for yourself.

Sit in your usual meditation posture. Take three deep breaths, fully inhaling and exhaling. If you like, you can let out your exhales with a big sigh, an audible "aahhhhh!"

Allow your heart center to open. You can do this by visualizing warm white or pink light enveloping the area around your chest, seeping in and energizing your heart. Or you can think of a loved one or anything that makes your heart come alive: a pile of puppies with big eyes playing together, a child in a meadow of flowers, whatever works for you.

Visualize yourself. You can see yourself as a baby or young child or as you are today, however you're able to hold an image of yourself with compassion.

Now say this mantra (in your head or aloud):

> May I be filled with loving kindness
>
> May I be healthy and well
>
> May I be safe in all ways
>
> May I be happy and at ease

Hold the feeling of love and compassion for yourself for a few breaths. You can repeat the mantra several times if you want or you can move on.

Now picture someone you love and are close to. Bring the feeling of them into your heart and mind and hold them there.

Say the mantra with them in mind:

> May you be filled with loving kindness

May you be healthy and well

May you be safe in all ways

May you be happy and at ease

Now bring to mind someone you feel neutral about, perhaps someone you don't know all that well, such as your mail carrier or the person who rings up your groceries at the store.

Visualize them and hold them in your heart and repeat the mantra again:

May you be filled with loving kindness

May you be healthy and well

May you be safe in all ways

May you be happy and at ease

Next, bring to your mind and heart someone you dislike or have a difficult relationship with, either in the past or present. It's OK if it feels difficult to hold them in a loving way and to repeat the mantra for them. Allow yourself to experience the feelings of discomfort you feel.

Repeat the mantra to them:

May you be filled with loving kindness

May you be healthy and well

May you be safe in all ways

May you be happy and at ease

Now move your awareness to your whole family as well as your neighborhood and/or local community. Include yourself as well and say the mantra again:

May we be filled with loving kindness

May we be healthy and well

May we be safe in all ways

May we be happy and at ease

Finally, zoom out in your consciousness and envelope the entire globe in your mind's eye, holding the Earth in your heart and repeat the mantra one last time:

May we be filled with loving kindness

May we be healthy and well

May we be safe in all ways

May we be happy and at ease

Here's a shorthand version of who you picture in each mantra:

- Yourself
- An easy, loving relationship

- A neutral relationship
- A difficult relationship
- Your neighborhood/community
- The world

Forgiveness visualization

If forgiving people who have hurt you feels like an overwhelming task that you're not up to handling alone, then it's time to call in some help. There's nothing wrong with asking for help—it's actually a sign of strength, rather than weakness.

Get into a quiet space within (by assuming your meditation posture, taking deep breaths, doing whatever you do to get calm inside and ready to connect with your inner self or Spirit). Ask one of the following to be with you to help you in your forgiveness work: your healer spirit guide, your higher self, God, Christ (or the Christ energy), your guardian angel, Buddha. It can be any entity you connect with that comes from pure light. Allow that energy to come and sit beside you.

While I'm not Christian, I feel a strong connection to Jesus Christ. I like the Unity philosophy of the Christ light within each of us. But if the idea of Jesus makes you shut down inside rather than open up, go

99

with something else. It can be John Lennon if that works for you.

As you sit with Jesus, Buddha, John, your angel or whoever, ask them to help you. First, ask them to help you forgive yourself. Imagine that your bearer of white light, a being filled with compassion and love, is holding you and looking into the very heart of you. They know all of your flaws and foibles, they see everything you've ever done, every lie you've told to yourself or others, every promise you've broken, every mean thing you've said or piece of gossip you've passed on and every jealous twinge you've felt and grudge you've held. And they love you, just as you are. They forgive you. Because they see your humanity and your full expression of Spirit in human form in this lifetime. Allow yourself to soak in this love and compassionate energy.

Together, invite the person you wish to forgive into your hearts. Ask your bearer of white light to help you see that person as they just saw you—with compassionate, loving, forgiving eyes and heart. If it becomes too hard for you to see your perpetrator with love, allow your higher being friend to help you.

Allow them to illuminate the goodness with that person so that you can find the compassion and love within yourself to forgive them.

Forgiveness work is hard. I'm not going to kid you. It's hard and it can be grueling and sometimes you might think you'll never ever possibly be done with it. (Or maybe that's just me.) But it's worth it. Forgiveness is such a worthwhile effort for how it can transform how you feel and think about yourself. This, in turn, transforms your vibration and your life. When it comes to raising your vibration, forgiving is a surefire way to do it.

Express gratitude

Gratitude raises your vibration, too.

Find the things in your life you're grateful for, no matter how small. In fact, it's often the small things in your life that have the biggest impact.

You can make this practice part of your daily life—feeling grateful for a perfectly brewed cup of tea or coffee, for your car starting on the first try (or the fifth), for a smile from someone on the sidewalk as you drive to work or school.

You can express gratitude for the people in your life and for some of the bigger things as well: having a roof over your head, a warm bed to sleep in, loved ones (even if you spend a lot of time and energy taking care of them), food to eat, enough money in the bank to pay the bills. Whatever good you've got going on in your life, notice it and allow yourself to feel gratitude for what you have, rather than worrying about what you don't.

You can also use or start a gratitude journal where you write down three things at the end of each day that you're grateful for. Or just one thing. Or you can do it in the morning when you wake up to set your intention for the day.

Another practice that works well for some people is to have a Happiness Jar. You write down one happening from the day on a slip of paper and date it with that day's date and put it in the jar. At the end of the year, you'll have a jar full of good moments in your life—which is a lot to be grateful for. You don't need to wait until January 1 to start your happiness or gratitude jar, you can start it today. It doesn't need to be fancy (although it can be if you want). And if you forget or skip days, you can just start again whenever you think of it.

Find things of beauty and contemplate them

This is closely related to gratitude, but can be done and expressed a little differently. There is so much beauty in our lives. It can be as simple as the way the sunlight falls through sheer curtains in your window. Or the perfect symmetry of a flower or the intricacy of nature. Or your child's face or the way the hair curls at the nape of her neck.

Give yourself permission to notice the beauty in life. Allow yourself the space and the time to slow down enough to literally stop and smell the roses.

Laugh

Laughter is a sure-fire way to raise your vibration. Spirit loves laughter. And it's great for your body and spirits.

So when the mood strikes you, laugh. And even if the mood doesn't strike you, you can raise your vibration by fake laughing. Or smiling. The act of moving your face into a smile formation releases neurochemicals in your brain that actually make you feel better. It's the same with laughter.

Listen to uplifting music

Music is an easy and wonderful way to raise your vibration. Put on some tunes that make you feel good—whether that's classical music that you can close your eyes and breathe deeply to or disco classics that make you want to dance around.

Obviously, songs with positive messages are going to raise your vibration more than songs about pain, violence and cheap sex. However, there are times when you may need to listen to music that helps release what you have going on inside you, and it's possible that you occasionally get into a place where heavy metal lifts you up at least a little bit higher than where you were. Use your discretion and listen to what your inner self really wants to hear and put that on.

Sing

It doesn't matter if you don't think you can sing, open your mouth and tra-la-laaaaaaa anyway. Singing, just like music, raises your vibration. That's why music and congregational singing is part of almost every church service. It raises your vibration and get it aligned with everyone else's and helps you be more open to receiving the message at the service.

So sing or hum or play and instrument. Create those sound vibrations in the universe and lift yours up at the same time.

Stop gossiping

Gossiping is a downer to everyone—the person speaking the gossip, the one hearing it and the person it's about. So stop doing it.

It can be hard to resist the temptation to gossip. I know this personally. But you can defeat the gossip monster. You can stop talking about other people behind their back—at the very least you can stop saying anything that you honestly wouldn't feel comfortable saying to their face.

To start, allow yourself to become aware of when the conversation turns to other people. Before you speak, ask yourself: Would you be OK saying this to that person? Is what you're going to share kind? Is it necessary? If not, stop. Don't say it. Steer the conversation down another path. You gain nothing by gossiping. Another person's downfall doesn't lift you up.

That doesn't mean you can't talk about other people who you are having difficult interactions with. But don't tear people down. Lift them up. You know the difference between an honest vent or trying to work through a tricky situation and gossip. Gossip feels different.

Do acts of kindness

Rather than gossip, be kind. Do acts of kindness. Randomly, on purpose, it doesn't matter. You can pick up garbage off the ground, give out clean socks to folks who are homeless, volunteer at a non-profit organization, tutor kids, pay for coffee for the person behind you in line, smile at strangers, stop for pedestrians who want to cross the road and yield whenever there's a dispute over a parking space.

Whenever you encounter a situation where you have a choice, choose the kind option. You won't lose. Nice guys do not finish last, as it turns out. Nice guys (of both the male and female genders) live longer, happier, more uplifting and fulfilling lives.

Kindness always wins (along with love).

Create a peaceful space in your life

I have a confession: I'm a messy person.

When I was 12 or 13, the floor of my bedroom was covered in so much stuff—clothes, magazines, books, who knows what—that you literally couldn't see the floor. I remember finally cleaning the room one day (my mother had taken to just keeping my door shut) and it felt so much better once it was all cleaned up. Even with that experience, I'm still messy, though never again that bad. We all have our challenges and things to work on. (In my defense, I also have 4 kids to clean up after who appear to take after me in this and many other ways).

Giving yourself a peaceful space to live and work is a blessing. It allows your mind to rest—which allows you to hear your inner voice more clearly.

So even if you can't tidy up and declutter your entire house, create a peaceful space for yourself where you can be and sit and rest your mind. That might become your meditation space. For me, it's the studio where I do my readings. I let myself bring my laptop in my studio so I can write (and a cup of tea so I'm awake enough to write), but nothing else. That way it doesn't get cluttered like my office or bedroom or dining room. There are no piles of bills or books to read or paperwork I'm procrastinating on either filing, throwing out or doing something with. It's a clear, clean space.

In addition to creating a peaceful physical space, create a time in your days where you can breathe, relax and go within. That may be just for a minute or two in between other events in your life, or it may be a regular practice at the same time each day. Do what you can.

Set and maintain boundaries

Here I go again with the boundaries. I'm a big believer in boundaries in all aspects of my life. Setting and maintaining your boundaries with people on this physical plane of existence will help you do the same when you're working with Spirit.

Know what's OK and not OK for you and love yourself enough to stick to it. That encompasses pretty much everything in your interpersonal relationships, including how you talk to and treat yourself and others and how you allow them to talk to you and treat you.

This may mean you end up needing to make changes in your life. There may be people around you that aren't good for you. And there may be things you're saying and doing (even just with yourself) that you need to change as well.

Hard as it sometimes is, knowing your boundaries and living in integrity with them will clear your energy and vibration right up. You'll be living authentically, which will then radiate from within you.

Chapter 7: Developing your intuitive abilities

> "If prayer is you talking to God, then intuition is God talking to you."
> —*Dr. Wayne Dyer*

Intuition is the foundation of mediumship. Developing your intuitive abilities is a vital step in living a life connected to Spirit. Intuition is, after all, a direct connection to Spirit—to your own higher self and the intelligent energy that manifests itself in all life.

What is intuition?

Intuition is defined as the ability to immediately understand something, without the need for conscious reasoning. Intuition is when you know something to be so because of instinctive feeling rather than conscious reasoning. The word itself is a late Middle English word that comes from the Latin *intueri*, which means "consider."

Intuition is often referred to as a still, small voice inside you. It's your inner voice. It's the voice of the God spark within you.

Listening to and developing your intuition is a topic that comes up over and over again in the readings I give. It's a big topic—and an important one—following your intuition can help you in so many areas of your life.

This is true for everyone—you can each safely rely on your intuition to help you have a better life—but especially so for folks wanting to develop their psychic, mediumship or healing abilities. A healthy and well-developed intuition is where it all begins. In fact, a huge part of being able to reliably give readings is based on your foundational trust in yourself and your intuition, as well as developing a relationship with your spirit guides.

How to develop your intuition

Intuition is something that grows as you feed it.

You may have heard the story between an elder and a boy—sometimes depicted as a Native American elder, often Cherokee, other times simply as a grandfather. The basics of the story is that the elder talks about the two wolves that live inside him, fighting for survival. One is full of anger, greed and hate. The other is peaceful and at ease, full of joy, love and wisdom.

The boy asks him, "Which one will win?" He answers, "The one I feed."

What we feed grows.

In some ways, developing your intuition is as simple as that. Give it time and nourishment and it will grow and flourish.

Your intuition is always talking to you and giving you information to get your feet on your highest path. It uses your mind, your body and all your senses to nudge you along, pushing and pulling you this way and that, giving you sudden insights and understanding that you can't pin on anything that makes sense.

Unfortunately, many of us stop trusting ourselves and our intuition somewhere along the way. Difficult things happen in your life, you get hurt, you feel lost and you become disconnected from your inner/higher self.

When you're in that state of unbalance, you often stop listening to your intuition. I know there have been blows in my life that have rocked me to the core.

When unexpected things happen and you're reeling in the aftermath, sometimes you go into survival mode and stop trusting your inner knowing. If this has happened to you, it's OK, you're totally normal (at least in that respect).

But there's hope. Even if your use of intuition is rusty, even if you've forgotten how to trust yourself, you can regain that knowledge and ability.

First steps

Get quiet inside

In order to hear the still, small voice inside you and help it become louder and clearer, you need to find ways to get quiet and still the mental chatter that takes up so much of your head space and drowns out your intuitive sense.

So, it'll come as no surprise when I suggest spending regular time in meditation of one kind or another. Remember, you can meditate while you're folding laundry, washing yourself in the shower, or walking around your neighborhood. It's often during these times when part of your attention is taken up by something else that intuitive insight will suddenly come to you in the form of an idea, an inspiration or the solution to a problem that you've been noodling on for a while.

Set your intention

In the Spiritualist church, at least at the one I learned mediumship in, when they talk about mediumship, they say, "mediumship gifts are open to everyone and can be developed through study and good intent." Intuition is the same.

Everyone has intuition and can access their intuition. It takes study and time. And it takes setting your intention.

You can do this in a formal or informal way. You can get out an intuition journal in which you'll record all your intuitive feelings and start it off with a statement of intent:

> I hereby declare my desire to open and connect with my intuition, knowing it will lead me on the path of my highest good.

Or you can say your intent out loud. You can tell a friend or family member with whom you can share such thoughts and ideas.

Or you can simply let the universe know that you're ready to step forward on your path of intuitively-led life and go from there.

However you do it, the idea is that you decide to start listening to your intuition and you make a commitment to yourself to do it. It's just like when you decide to do anything new—to start a diet or exercise program, look for a job, learn a new skill. You make a commitment to do something differently, and then you take the steps.

Write down your dreams and synchronicities

Your dreams could be telling you something. Even if they're not profound prophetic dreams, they're a way to get in touch with your emotional self and what you're working out on the inside.

Don't think you dream? You do. We all do (or we'd go insane). But you may not be remembering them when you wake up. You can start remembering your dreams again—and if you already remember some things, you can increase the amount you remember.

If you don't remember any of your dreams, when you relax in bed at night before going to sleep, set the intention that you'll remember your dreams when you wake up.

If you remember some of your dreams when you wake up, at least some of the time, write down whatever it is that you can recall as soon as you wake up enough to hold a pen (or open your laptop). The more you do this, the better your recall will become.

You don't necessarily need to analyze your dreams or do anything with your dream journal. Simply opening up to this part of yourself will help activate and increase your intuitive abilities.

You can also write down the synchronicities you notice happening in your life. These are the things that could be coincidences but feel like something more. The moments when you know who's calling or texting you before you look at the phone, or when you bump into or hear from someone who you've been thinking about. Or when you've been wondering about something, trying to come up with a solution or answer, and it suddenly presents itself to you—whether that's in the form of a sudden thought that comes to you or in a news article that someone happens to post on Facebook that shows up in your feed.

Write them down. It'll help build your confidence that something real is happening.

Awaken your intuitive body

Your body is the vessel that houses your soul so it can experience life in physical form. And, no matter how you may feel about it, it's truly your friend.

Your intuitive body tries to help you out in so many ways—some of which you may not appreciate at the time—by giving you signals about whether what you're doing with your life is working for you or not. Some of those signals are gentle nudges—a headache or stomachache when life is more stressful than is good for you or you need to make a difficult decision. Others are the proverbial spiritual 2x4 to the head: your back goes out or you break a bone so you're forced to take a break and do things differently.

You can awaken and tune into your intuitive body through the mindfulness exercise later in this chapter and then go on to use your intuitive body as a tool to help you make decisions for your highest good.

Ultimately, your intuitive body will help you in mediumship work by giving you signals such as how a person in Spirit died and what illness or injuries they had while they were in physical form. You can also receive information about the person you're doing a reading for (or yourself) in terms of where they have energy blockages—or great, free-flowing energy—or potential areas of concern with their health.

Make friends with your body

If you've struggled with chronic illness or pain or have had to recover from injury, you may feel like your body has betrayed you. I speak from personal experience here as I cannot actually remember a time in my life when I didn't have chronic pain. I've had back pain of one kind or another since I was about 12 and headaches before that. Initially my back pain was from scoliosis, then from three bulging discs due to a car accident when I was a teenager. That led to the development of fibromyalgia and multiple chemical sensitivities and migraines in my late teens and 20 years of chronic pain. Eventually, I had spinal fusion on my lumbar spine (which really helped). My health seems to go through up and down cycles, yet here I am, still living in this physical body and having gestated and birthed two awesome healthy children.

I'm telling you this abbreviated medical history so that I can explain why, for a long time, I felt betrayed by my body. There were so many things I wanted to do that I couldn't do. I felt stymied and re-strained by the very vessel I was supposed to be living my life through. It wasn't until a spiritual counselor recommended that I make friends with my pain (this was before I'd decided to have back surgery) that it clicked. My pain and illness isn't my enemy. I don't have to fight it. My body is not against me. It's for me and it always has been. It's on my side.

What my body was trying to tell me when I was younger and having headaches was that something was wrong. My intuition knew that things weren't right in my life. It knew there were things happening to me that needed to come to light and be dealt with. And it was true, there were—mostly in the form of repressed sexual abuse.

But it didn't get dealt with.

And so my body started sending ever more urgent warning messages.

When I developed fibromyalgia, it stopped me dead in my tracks from continuing down a path that could have been disastrous for me (it basically involved lots of bad teenage decisions including sex, drugs and rock 'n' roll). Good news—it finally got my attention.

And throughout the years since, my body has continued to give me signals that say, "Hey, pay attention to this, look at this, do things differently. Please." I've finally gotten smart enough to listen.

Today, when I get signals from my body—whether it's in the form of a headache or heartburn—I pay attention. I get quiet inside and ask my body what's going on, what I need to know, how I need to move forward. I'm not perfect at it. I still get frustrated. I still want to push too hard and try to do too much when what I need to do is slow down a little and rest, but I know better. I'm no longer at war with my body. I respect it. I treat it kindly and I try and say nice things to it and nourish it, rather than abuse and neglect it.

Intuitive body mindfulness exercise

This exercise takes a couple of minutes at most and can be done pretty much anywhere if you need to. You can even do it with your eyes open, although you may prefer to close your eyes so that you can tune in more deeply with your body.

- Sit quietly and comfortably. Take three deep breaths—inhaling fully and exhaling completely (breathing in through your nose and

120

breathing out either through your nose or mouth).

- Notice your body. How does it feel right now?

- Do a scan of your body, limiting your thoughts, emotions and judgements about what you feel as much as possible. Are there areas of your body that your attention is drawn to? Is there aching or stiffness? Areas that feel good and energized? Areas that just are and don't particularly feel one way or another?

- Acknowledge your body and the role it plays in enabling you to experience a physical existence.

- Thank your body for everything it has given you—the illness and aches and limitations as well as the blessing of life.

- Make a pact with your body that you will listen to what it tells you.

Using your intuitive body to connect with your inner knowing

Once you've made friends with your body to the best of your ability at this time, you can strengthen your relationship by actively seeking its input and participation in your life.

Your intuitive body will give you information about whether or not you're on the right track. You're probably familiar with the term "gut feeling." Well, that's your intuitive body talking to you through your stomach or gut.

Consider a decision you're facing. It can be about anything: moving to a new house, starting or leaving a relationship, changing jobs or asking for a raise, deciding to have a child, taking a risk in some area of your life. Whatever it is that you're pondering lately.

- Find a quiet spot where you won't be interrupted for 5-10 minutes.
- Put some meditative music on if you like, or just sit in silence and become aware of the sounds around you, without focusing on any of them in particular.
- Breathe deeply and quiet your body and your mind.
- Ask Spirit to guide you. I usually begin these types of meditations (yes, you're meditating!) with a short prayer, something like: *Hey, Spirit, I'm here. I'm open to knowing what I*

need to know today, for my highest and best good.

- Think about your decision for a moment or two. Keep breathing deeply. Know the answers you need are available to you.

- Think about one outcome of your decision as if it is the reality of your life right now. Put yourself in that moment.

- How does it feel in your body? What sensations do you notice? Does it feel heavy in your chest or stomach, or light and clear? Does your breath get tight and short or does it come easily, with relief? Are there muscles that get tight? Does your head start to hurt?

- Think about the other option and its outcome, as if it is your life in the present moment. How does that feel?

- Let go of both options and quietly consider your intuitive feelings. One of the two (or three, or four) potential outcomes will feel best to you.

Awaken your intuitive feet

This exercise combines exercise, meditation and tapping into your intuition all together! It's a three-for-one deal. And it's simple.

Put on your shoes and step outside. Breathe. Take a walk to nowhere in particular. Just let your feet lead you. You can start your walk by giving direction to your feet if you like: *intuitive feet, lead me where I need to go today*.

Walk. Turn where you are led. Notice what you see. Notice where you feel moved to go.

Be quietly open, but don't push for confirmation. You're not trying to prove anything or go anywhere profound. Perhaps nothing happens, and that's OK.

Awaken your intuitive senses

Just as you have five physical senses of sight, sound, taste, touch and smell, you also have intuitive senses (lumped together, these would be considered your sixth sense). Your intuitive senses are the underpinnings of the clairsenses: clairvoyance (sight), clairaudience (sound), clairgustience (taste) and clairalience (smell). (Claircognizance and clairsentience are related to your intuitive mind, body and heart.)

Activating your intuitive senses will help your mediumship abilities flourish. Here are some fun activities you can incorporate into your daily life to awaken each of your intuitive senses. The next book in this series goes into opening your intuitive or psychic senses in depth.

The purpose of these exercises isn't so much the outcome (although those may delight and surprise you) as it is establishing and building a relationship with your intuition in lots of different ways. Relationships take time and trust to build. These activities and exercises build trust with your intuitive self over time.

Intuitive seeing: The what to wear game

When you get dressed for the day, rather than grabbing whatever is clean and nearby, or obsessing over the right thing, stop for a moment and ask your intuition to guide you.

Look at your clothing options. What items stand out most to you? Which appear brighter somehow, or pull at your attention or tug you in some way? Ask your intuition what color you should wear.

Put on whatever you feel drawn to. Then relax.

You may notice, if you're going to a place where there will be a number of people (like an office or a gathering of some kind) that you're wearing the same color shirt or outfit as several other people. You may have someone compliment your outfit. Perhaps nothing at all of note will happen, and that's OK, too. By allowing your intuitive eyes to pick out your outfit, you're awakening them and letting them know you're paying attention and listening.

Intuitive hearing: Who is calling?

The next time your phone rings, before you look at the caller ID, ask your intuition who's calling you. Whose voice do you hear? Whose name pops into your head?

Or when you're listening to the radio or streaming music, are there lyrics in songs that stand out to you? If so, ask your intuition what they mean and why you're hearing them right at that moment.

Just like with picking out your clothes, there's nothing huge at stake here. It doesn't matter if you're right or wrong. It's just a game to gently open up access to your intuition.

Intuitive tasting: What should I eat?

Your taste buds are intuitive, too. Or, rather, your body knows what it needs to be healthy and well.

If you're out to eat somewhere, while you're looking at the menu, ask your intuition what you should choose to eat. What feels intuitively right to your taste buds (or your entire body)? You can do this even before you see the menu—while choosing the restaurant and deciding on what kind of flavors of food are right for you to eat for that meal.

Intuitive smelling: Something smells fishy here

You've heard the phrases, "something smells fishy" and "I smell a rat," right? They're prime examples of how you use your intuition, even when you don't realize it. To open up your intuitive sense of smell, you don't need to literally go around sniffing things out. Just be aware of any signals your intuitive nose might give you. If there's something that somehow "smells off" in a situation in your life, trust your intuition and look deeper. Be open and see what comes up.

Awaken your intuitive mind

Information you receive through your intuitive mind is similar to claircognizance, "clear knowing." It comes through as a sudden, clear flash of thought or inspiration. Where do you think ideas come from, anyway? They're intuitive inspiration.

In order to receive intuitive information in your mind, your mind needs to be clear. It needs a chance to get quiet and reasonably empty. It needs to stop churning. All the previously mentioned ways of getting clear and quiet and raising your vibration will help your intuitive mind awaken and be open.

One of my favorite ways to allow intuition to work in my life through my intuitive mind, especially when I'm stuck on a problem, is to go for a walk. I'll begin the walk with that problem in mind and, by the time I return home (or to my car if I drove somewhere to start my walk), the solution will have presented itself in some way to me—usually as a flash of insight as I put one foot in front of the other.

Sometimes I actively work on the problem as I walk. I ask myself questions. I delve into what's making me anxious about it or why I'm feeling stuck. I ask Spirit for help. I ask why this situation is in my life right now. And then I get distracted by the trees or another thought in my mind, or I simply let the rhythm of my feet taking step after step soothe me and allow my mind to relax in a walking meditation. At some point, solutions appear.

And, should I somehow find myself back where I started my walk without a resolution of some kind, I know that the universe and my higher self are working on it and the answer will be delivered to me when it's ready. That usually happens the next time my mind is in a peaceful state—just before I fall asleep or wake up, when I'm in the shower, or when I'm in a half-zoned out state while spinning yarn on my spinning wheel or even while I'm playing Candy Crush on my phone.

Once you receive intuitive insight, act on it. This builds your trust in yourself and connects the pathways of your intuition so they become stronger.

Awaken your intuitive heart

Your intuitive heart is closely connected to the rest of your intuitive self. I think of it as the center of your love and trust.

To awaken your intuitive heart, you need to decide to start trusting yourself and your intuition. You need to believe that your highest good is possible. Your intuitive heart is a source of compassion and healing, for yourself and others and for the world around you.

Begin making decisions from your heart, rather than your head. The intuitive journey is one of trust. You'll begin to know and do things that don't necessarily make rational sense. But they make heart sense, they make intuitive sense, and that's the important thing.

Give yourself time

Developing any skill or ability takes time. So give yourself time, space and permission to take as long as you need to unfold your intuition. Especially if you've recently been through a difficult period in your life, where you've instinctively gone into survival mode and plowed on through, or are coming out of a period of depression and self-doubt. Give yourself time. When you've been emotionally tightly curled in a ball or flexing your armor-covered muscles, it takes a bit to relax and unfurl and be emotionally vulnerable enough to get quiet and listen to yourself again.

Also, give yourself as many opportunities as you can to listen to and develop your intuition. You can use your intuition for decisions big and small. Go inside, tune into your inner knowledge and make decisions from your heart and gut. Do this over and over and over again to build your intuition and your trust in it.

Chapter 8: Opening and closing to Spirit

When you think of developing your mediumship abilities, you might think about how you can be open to information from Spirit. One of the things I'd like you to consider is that you also need to know how to close the door on that information as well.

In fact, for many folks interested in mediumship and developing their abilities, the problem isn't so much how to be open to Spirit, it's that you are too wide open and don't know how to control or stop the flow of information.

If you're one of those people who sees and senses Spirit and other people's emotions when you don't want to, it's OK. It doesn't have to be this way. You can remain connected to Spirit and be in control of how and when you receive information.

If you don't feel like you see and sense Spirit as much as you'd like, that's OK, too. Learning how to open and close to Spirit will help you connect in a better, stronger way.

I'm going to give you some opening and closing techniques which will help you take control of your connection with Spirit—saying a prayer of intent, installing a hatch in the crown of your head, and creating physical cues.

A prayer of intent

You know by now that your intent is powerful when it comes to working with Spirit. I begin each session, class or circle with a prayer of intent. This sets the tone for what's about to happen and also asks Spirit for what I need.

The prayer can be pretty much anything. For readings with my clients, I usually say something along the lines of:

> Gracious Spirit, Infinite Intelligence, I ask that I am an open and clear medium for (person's name) to bring them messages that are useful, uplifting and what they need to hear and know right here and now for their highest and best good. I ask this in all honesty and sincerity. My door is open. And so it is.

For a class or circle, it goes something like:

> Gracious Spirit, Infinite Intelligence,
> thank you for bringing us together today
> so that we may learn and grow together,
> in a nurturing, supportive circle. Help us
> have the courage to give out the mes-
> sages we receive, knowing that only the
> highest and best good comes to us. Our
> doors are open. And so it is.

Basically, I ask for what we need. And then I state that my doors are open. I do this along with the visualization technique in the next section of this chapter.

At the end of a circle or class, I say another short prayer, to close. In it, I'll thank Spirit for the learning we shared together, ask Spirit to be with us and guide our steps until we meet again and then end with, "our doors are closed."

At the end of a reading, I'm less formal. I tell my client that I leave all that I've shared with them in love and light, and that the people they brought with them get to home with them and can't stay with me.

Install and use a hatch

My students sometimes look at me like I've slightly lost my mind when I first explain this technique to them—and yet it works, so give it a try. This technique uses visualization to consciously open and close yourself to Spirit.

Imagine a hatch on the top of your skull, right on your crown chakra. It's able to open and close, directed by your will and intent. It can be like a trapdoor that opens up out of the top of your skull. It can be a sliding hatch that retracts into your skull. Go with whatever image works for you. This is the door I refer to in my opening and closing prayers.

If you find you can't just think a hatch there, visualize a spirit guide creating it in your skull with white light (like some kind of white light laser). Imagine pure energy from Infinite Intelligence, the source of all that is, entering the top of your skull like a laser cutter. First it cuts one side of the hatch, then the second, then the third (the fourth is like a hinge, at least in my head). Fill your crown chakra with this white light. Feel its warmth and let it relax and open your door.

When I want to connect with Spirit, I say one of my opening prayers and visualize the door opening. When I've finished, I visualize the door closing, back down into my skull.

Give Spirit signals

Do you remember the grounding technique I taught you where you lock your feet into the ground? These physical signals are similar: they're a signal to Spirit that you're either ready for the juices to start flowing or that you're all done and are no longer open to communication.

When I begin a reading, I rub my hands together. It's become an automatic gesture and I find myself doing it even without thinking about it. It's one of the techniques I learned when I first studied mediumship. My teacher had us go into a meditative, almost hypnotic, state and imprinted the suggestion of a gesture that would help us automatically connect with Spirit whenever we do it.

This gesture could be anything—tapping your right knee with your fingers, crossing your toes, touching your left arm. For me, it was rubbing my hands together. Ask Spirit what would work well for you, or just decide on something and basically say,

"Hey, whenever I do this thing, that means I'm ready for communication to come through, OK?" Don't make it overly complicated. Rubbing your palms together works just fine. It also has the happy side-effect of helping to raise energy if you're not feeling a good connection.

To close my connection with Spirit, in addition to visualizing the trap door in my head closing, I've found I sweep my arms through the air in a shooing gesture, as if I'm shooing the folks in Spirit who have come through back out the door. Do you know the New Year's Eve tradition of opening the doors and windows in your house at midnight, to welcome in the New Year and shoo out the old year and its energy? It's something we did every year when I was a kid and I loved the ritual. I think of that when I sweep out the energy of the folks who've come to visit.

Only being open when you want to

If you find that you're susceptible to seeing Spirit when you don't mean to be, you need to get stronger at setting your intentions and boundaries. Remember that you're in control of this experience. You have free will. You don't have to talk to people in Spirit if you don't want to. And if you do, you are allowed to do it on your terms.

If it feels like Spirit is being pushy, it helps to have a regular day and time when you are open to Spirit communication. That way, you can say, "I'm open Tuesdays at 2 p.m. Come and see me then," or "Spirit hours are during meditation at 10 a.m."

If you get woken up a lot during the night, feeling like someone in Spirit is trying to communicate with you, you can ask them to stop. One of my students puts up a "Closed" sign on her bedroom door at night. Another has learned to ask her Gatekeeper guide (more on that in chapter 9) to guard her at night and not let Spirit entities through.

The more you practice intentionally opening and closing to Spirit communication, the better you get at it. It also becomes easier to discern if you're in an open or closed state and adjust accordingly.

Remember that you only need to receive communication that feels good to you and is for your highest and best good. And even if your closed sign is up for communication with Spirit entities, you're still connected to your intuition and inner guidance.

Chapter 9:
Your spirit guides

Folks interested in developing their mediumship skills often have questions about spirit guides. They often include:

- What are they?
- How many do you have?
- Do they change over time?
- Can they be deceased family members or friends?
- How do you know who yours are?
- How do you meet them, get to know them and receive guidance from them?

Depending on who you ask, there are lots of different—often conflicting—answers to these questions.

My approach to mediumship and spirituality is: what works for you, works for you. What resonates with you is your truth. You know the feeling of hearing your personal truth: it's like a bell rings inside you vibrating at the same frequency as you do, or you suddenly well up with tears you didn't know you had. Go with it.

What are spirit guides?

Spirit guides are considered to be ethereal entities (beings not in physical bodies) who are around to help you in some way. Many people consider them separate entities from you: beings that have existed for eons and have evolved to help others, ascended angels or even aliens.

Here's what I think: the entities we connect with and call our spirit guides are really aspects of our own higher selves. They are us. They are a way we conceptualize our own soul and connect with it to gain wisdom, knowledge and clarity.

In general, when it comes to spirituality, we externalize and look for meaning and connection with something outside ourselves. Yet everything we need can be found within. We are connected to everything that is in this universe, we are part of one mind—the universal life force energy that makes up everything on this planet and in existence.

Thinking of your spirit guides as distinct entities helps them make sense to you, just as the concept of linear time helps you make sense of your life. But consider that they are really a part of you, of your own soul or higher self that is so much more expansive than you can understand while in a physical body.

Externalizing the idea of spirit guides and making them something outside of yourself is a way of being able to understand them and connect with them. Imagine if I said to you, "Hey, it's time to have a conversation with your soul. Let your soul guide you and protect you." It's such an intangible, abstract thing, thinking about the nature of your soul, that it's hard to really connect with it in a meaningful way.

However, imagine I said, "This is Ralph. He's your guide. He's here to help you on your path. He's got long, shoulder-length hair and he's wearing a tie-dye t-shirt with a peace symbol on it. He's smiling and welcoming you to sit down next to him." Can you imagine that, your sweet, peaceful hippie spirit guide wanting to have a chat with you?

Whether you prefer to think of your spirit guides as excarnate spiritually evolved beings separate from you or as aspects of your own divine self, it doesn't really matter in terms of how you get to know them and work with them. Either way, they're on your side and here to help you grow and learn and become the most fully actualized, authentic version of yourself that you can be.

How many spirit guides do you have?

Different books and different people say vastly different things about the number of spirit guides you have.

Some say you have two guides: a master guide and another guide. Some say you have just one. Others teach that you have an inner band of guides that stays the same and an outer band who change over time.

I was taught you have a band of seven guides—gatekeeper, teacher, doctor, philosopher, native, master teacher and joy guide.

Are you confused yet? Does it really matter how many spirit guides you have? I don't think it does. I think it might be different for different people, depending on their needs and where they are in their spiritual journey. If your guides are reflections and aspects of your own higher self, then you have as many as you need or are able to understand you have at the point in time you're at.

Do spirit guides change over time?

Some people say yes, others say no. I say: not really.

Friends and loved ones in your physical life come and go. Some people are with you for decades (such as your parents or siblings) while others are around for a few years or months. Could it be the same with your spirit guides?

My guides (facets of my higher self) have stayed fairly constant over the past 15 years, with certain aspects coming to the forefront as I work on different skills, e.g. healing work or mediumship. But since your guides are actually part of you, rather than separate from you, then while they may change over time, taking on different personas and faces, they are still ultimately the same.

The important thing to know is that you can never be abandoned by your guides. They'll always be there for you as they are part of your own higher self.

Can your loved ones become your spirit guides?

Yes. And no.

My mother is currently acting as a guide. It's what she needs to do as the next part of her journey, and I've decided to let her. Yet she's not an aspect of my own higher self. Will she be a spirit helper for me forever? I don't know. It's nice having her around (and she's much less pushy and judgmental in Spirit). But, just as her role in my physical life changed over time as I grew up, her role in my spiritual life is likely to change as well.

My brother, Anthony, is also closely connected with me and acts very much in a guiding and protective capacity. But he's not really one of my spirit guides. He's more like a big brother in Spirit, which is what he is.

I believe that friends and loved ones in Spirit step in from time to time to connect and help out in their behind-the-scenes way. They'll forever be connected to you, but aren't always at the forefront of your spiritual journey and learning. Your guides are.

Meeting your spirit guides

Meditation is the best way I know of to connect with your spirit guides. No surprise, I know.

Here's my favorite guided meditation to meet one or more of your spirit guides. You can record the text in your own voice and play it back during the meditation, you can have a friend read it to you, or you can read it beforehand and hold the steps in your mind. Once you've gone through it, it becomes easier to repeat it by yourself whenever you'd like to connect with your guides or meet more of them.

Spirit guide meditation

Imagine white light filling your body with every exhalation. With every inhalation, all anxiety, stress and tension leaves your body. As you exhale, you are filled with light, from your root chakra, building and growing as it travels up your spine, up to your crown chakra and out of the top of your skull.

See yourself standing at the foot of a staircase.

Begin to climb up the stairs. One step, then another.

See yourself climbing higher and higher.

145

As you approach the top of the stairway, you see a door. It gets closer and closer and then you are in front of it.

In your hand, there is a key. Put the key into the lock on the door and turn it. The door unlocks.

You open the door and step across the threshold, to the world on the other side. You see a place of beauty that resonates deeply within you.

Continue moving forward in this place.

In the distance, you see a figure moving toward you. This is one of your spirit guides. As they get closer, take in their appearance and the energy that they carry with them. Make a mental note of this feeling so you can recognize it when you return. Feel the warmth of the tremendous love they have for you.

As you approach each other, greet them. Sit down together or go for a walk.

Ask them about the role they play in your life. You can talk, or just be together.

When it feels like time to leave, ask them for a way to connect with them again—some kind of identifying characteristic such as a name, a symbol or even just a color.

Thank your guide.

See the door you came through. Step back through the doorway and close the door behind you, knowing you can return any time you'd like.

Step down the staircase, one step at a time, until you reach the bottom and return back to the chair you are sitting in. Become aware of your body, wiggle your fingers and toes, and open your eyes, feeling awake and energized.

You can go back to this meditation anytime you'd like to check in with your guides (although you don't need to unlock the door in subsequent visits). The more time you spend with your guides, the stronger relationships you build and the easier it is to connect with them and receive information from them. You can also call on them when you do mediumship or healing work.

Developing a relationship with your guides

Your relationship with your spirit guides develops much like any other relationship—with time, patience and effort.

Check in with them regularly—through meditation and even just through thought and intent.

147

When you're working on mediumship development, one of the important guides to get to know and develop a good relationship with is your gatekeeper. I call him my bouncer guide—he's the one who lines people up in Spirit when I'm doing readings, keeps them in line, and boots any troublemakers.

He's also who I can call on if I'm being bothered by folks in Spirit, either because they're showing up when I don't want them to, or because they are stepping in too strongly and causing me physical discomfort (sometimes people in Spirit are determined to let you know how they died by giving you strong physical sensations which can be quite unpleasant to experience). I also work with my gatekeeper to make stronger connections with folks in Spirit if they are not coming through clearly.

If I'm doing healing work, then I connect in with my healing guide and ask her to step forward to direct my hands and help me connect deeply to healing energy from Spirit.

The key here is that I ask them to step in when I need them. This goes back to your intent and consciously setting your intention.

One of the great things about working with your spirit guides is that they are timeless relationships.

You can pick up from where you left off and there's no jealousy or misunderstanding. The love between you is unconditional.

Signs and symbols from Spirit and your guides

As you begin working with your guides, it can be helpful to establish or develop some signs or symbols so that you know the information you're receiving is coming from them, or you know you're on the right path.

You can choose any kind of symbol—a song, a flower, an animal, a sequence of numbers—to let you know you're connecting with them and on the right track.

That's your code word with Spirit.

You can keep it simple, or you can go a little deeper. You can ask your guides to give you specific signs or symbols if you're on the right track and other signs if you're on the wrong track. Seeing sequences of repeating or increasing numbers, for instance, such as 11:11, 123, 6789, etc., can indicate that you're on the right path and should continue with the idea or project that you have in mind or are working on.

Decreasing sequences of numbers, accompanied by your own intuition, can indicate that you're not on track.

As you work with signs from your guides, you'll start to find them showing up more and more in your life. To choose a sign or symbols, you can ask your guides what they'd like to use or pick something that somehow feels meaningful to you. One of my symbols is a dragonfly, for instance, as it's come up in my life over and over again and resonates with me.

Chapter 10: Interpreting messages and symbols

Contrary to how it might look on TV, mediumship often isn't quite as simple as opening a connection with Spirit and spouting whatever comes through. It takes energy for people in Spirit to communicate with people in physical form.

While the connection and information sometimes comes through loud and clear, easy to understand and to the point, often information from Spirit comes through in symbolic form. Symbols are the way that Spirit talks to you—through your dreams, in flashes of vision, in song lyrics and even in the things you see in your everyday life such as flowers, insects and birds.

Spirit uses symbols to communicate with you because it takes less energy. Symbols are something you're intimately familiar with, as they are the way you already interact with your environment. The words you're reading right now are themselves symbols, each with a sound that, grouped together into a word, confers a specific meaning. (It gets a bit trippy if you think about it too hard.)

Symbols are a form of psychic or intuitive shorthand. And, to further the energy conservation, symbolic messages often pack a two-for-one punch. If a symbol comes through connected to a person, as a way of identifying that person, it often also is part of the message from that person. For instance, if you see a person working with their hands and, along with other information you receive, you're able to use that image to identify the person in Spirit (say, someone's uncle who was a mechanic), the message may also be related to the symbology of hands. It could be that the person you're receiving the message for needs to be more hands-on in their work, or that they'll be pursuing a career that uses their hands in some way.

How you receive symbols

You can receive symbolic information in all kinds of ways—basically in all the same ways you receive information from Spirit: through seeing, hearing, smelling, tasting, feeling and knowing.

You might see certain symbols physically with your literal eyes or in your mind's eye. They may come as images in dreams, something you see in nature or an image in a magazine. You may see a certain symbol during meditation, especially if you're asking for information from Spirit about a person or situation. A medium I know sees words and names written out in her mind's eye.

You can receive symbolic information through sound, as well. Perhaps you catch a line of dialogue on the radio or TV or overhear a snippet of conversation that resonates within you and wakes up an intuitive insight. Or you hear a song on the radio whose lyrics gives you a sudden insight. If you're clairaudient, you may also hear words or songs during a mediumship reading. You might also receive a symbol in the form of a single word that you hear with your intuitive ears.

The same goes for information that comes through taste and smell. Sometimes the information is literal: you smell the tang of a lemon being squeezed to make lemonade (often information comes through using more than one sense), which is connected to someone in Spirit who used to often make fresh lemonade. Again, the message from that person may be connected to the symbol through which they're identified (making the best out of a situation, perhaps).

In terms of symbolic information that comes through feeling or knowing, it often shows up in a quick flash. Often this information is more literal than symbolic—it's a direct knowing or understanding that doesn't need a lot of interpretation. You know a loved one is in trouble, perhaps, or that your grandmother is about to pass into Spirit.

Most often, symbols come through using a variety of your senses. You may get the sense of water, for instance, through a combination of feeling a cool mist on your skin and the taste of salt on your tongue, as well as the scent of the ocean. Using your intuition, you can ask what it means and where it is, to get a sense that it's by the ocean and the water is renewing and refreshing the person going through it, washing away their past emotions.

Working with and interpreting symbols

When you make a conscious decision to start working with symbols, you'll find that they start showing up in your life and your mediumship practice. You'll begin to get more information through symbols, which will deepen your connection with Spirit and the meaning of the messages themselves. Because it's an easier, quicker way for Spirit and your guides to connect with you, you'll begin to get more useful information transmitted symbolically.

Remember how I suggested you come up with some specific signs or symbols to communicate with your guides about whether or not you're on the right track? Well, by doing that, you're creating your own language with which you communicate with Spirit.

By working with symbols, you continue to create that language.

The next step is to define what the symbols that most commonly show up for you mean. This allows you to expand your language database with Spirit, which causes the information you get to be more reliable and consistent. Both you and folks in Spirit don't have to work quite as hard for the information to come through.

For instance, if you've received the symbol of an empty baby's crib and have, through questioning (both Spirit and the person you're giving the message to) determined that this image is connected with a child or baby who died, then the next time that image shows up, you can save everyone a lot of work by recognizing what it means. You see (or otherwise sense) an empty crib and you know that you're connecting with someone who passed into Spirit while still in the womb, as a baby or as a young child.

One way to do this in a proactive manner is to create your own symbol dictionary. You can do this by using a blank journal or an alphabetized book (like an address book, perhaps), or by purchasing *The Spiritual Symbols Workbook: Create your own dictionary of intuitive, psychic and metaphysical symbols* which takes a lot of the work out of it for you by already having more than 1,500 common symbols, categorized and alphabetized. (Disclaimer: I wrote *The Spiritual Symbols Workbook*.)

You can begin working with your symbol dictionary by writing down the symbols that come to you and the meanings you intuit about them. You can also use dream or psychic symbol dictionaries to give you an idea of the archetypal meaning and see if that resonates with you or not. If it does, write down your own interpretation. If it doesn't, then ask your intuition and guides what it means for you.

It's OK if a symbol means something different to you than it does to anyone else. A single symbol may also have more than one meaning, as well. Take a rose, for example. The sweet scent of a rose connects me to my mother. A blooming rose means that things are opening up and good is coming my way. But a rose with a stem has thorns, which means to watch out for hidden dangers. At least to me, it does. It might mean something different to you, and that's completely normal.

That's because we all have filters.

Understanding your filter

Your filter is the lens through which you experience the world. Your lens is created by the sum total of all your experiences: what languages you speak and the cultures you grew up and have been exposed to, including the TV shows you've watched, music you've listened to and food you've eaten, as well as places you've visited, activities you've tried and books you've read.

These experiences form a sort of internal database of all your known experiences.

Spirit uses this database to communicate with you in a language you can understand. It's not often you get symbols of things you've never seen before (although occasionally I get information for other people in languages I don't speak, they are still languages whose existence I know of).

What this means is that you'll see symbols that are familiar to you, especially if you are working on your own internal symbol dictionary while developing your intuition or understanding your dreams. If you're doing intuitive or psychic readings for others, then you may see things from their internal database of experiences that are unfamiliar to you, or from that of their loved one if you're practicing mediumship. However, for the most part, you're going to be working with symbols that you've encountered before, at one time or another, in some context.

The more you work with your symbols and strengthen your connection to what they mean to you, the more Spirit will use those symbols with your interpretations during whatever work you're doing.

Knowing if a symbol is from Spirit

One of the questions I'm asked most often in terms of symbols and signs from Spirit is how you can know if it's real or if it's your imagination.

There are two markers I've found that come into play when a symbol is from Spirit: repetition and a feeling of divine connection.

If there is a symbol that you see multiple times, especially when you think of a specific loved one or situation, then that's a sign from Spirit. Sometimes it can be obvious: you've been thinking about learning a new skill or taking a class and two different people mention that skill and then you happen to read an article about it as well, all within days of each other.

The other marker is a feeling of divine connection. There's a feeling that happens within you when a certain symbol comes into your experience that only happens when the symbol is from Spirit. For instance, my mother often comes through with the symbol of a rose—either in the form of a physical rose or the scent of one. However, I see roses all the time. I probably see dozens of roses every single day—there are several bushes growing in my garden, plus all the ones I drive by in the car or see on TV as well as a silk arrangement I have on my piano. But I don't think of my mother or feel her energy every time I walk down my front walk to the car. At certain times, my attention will be drawn to a certain rose, or I'll get a waft of rose scent on the air and, at the same time, I will think of her, see her smile or feel her warmth and love. That's when it's a true connection with Spirit.

Most of all, trust yourself. Trust your intuition and your inner knowing. If it feels like a connection, then it is.

Chapter 11: Moving forward

So now what? Where do you go from here?

Unfolding your mediumship skills takes time. And practice. And patience.

Treat yourself well—take care of your body, settle your mind and work on clearing up the issues in your life as best as you can.

This book and the exercises within it should give you a good grounding and foundation in the beginnings of your mediumship abilities—how to consciously open and close yourself to information from Spirit, how to raise/clear your vibration and quiet your mind enough to receive information, and how to begin making sense of it.

The next book in this series covers specific aspects of mental mediumship. If you'd like to know when it's available and find out more about me, visit my website at www.alightintuition.com where you can sign up for my mailing list and learn more about mediumship, energy healing and intuition.

Acknowledgements

I'm so grateful to the National Spiritualist Association of Churches, Plymouth Spiritualist Church and the Morris Pratt Institute, all of which provided me a valuable education in mediumship. I've benefitted so much from a number of teachers over the last 16 years, as well as the invaluable and sweet friendships with many of my peers.

I must also acknowledge my students and clients, who teach me at least as much as I teach them.

More from this author

Rev. Joanna Bartlett is an ordained Spiritualist minister and certified medium through the National Spiritualist Association of Churches. She lives in Eugene, Oregon, where she mentors students, teaches classes on intuition and mediumship and sees clients.

She's the author of:

The Spiritual Symbols Workbook: Create your own dictionary of intuitive, psychic and metaphysical symbols

Intuitive Symbols Coloring Book: Unlock your intuition through meditative coloring

The Awesomely Amazing Adventures of Cherry: Butterfly Buddies, a children's novel about friendship, grief and learning to speak your truth.

Learn more at www.alightintuition.com.

Index

Index

Made in the USA
Columbia, SC
17 July 2021